ROCK SETS

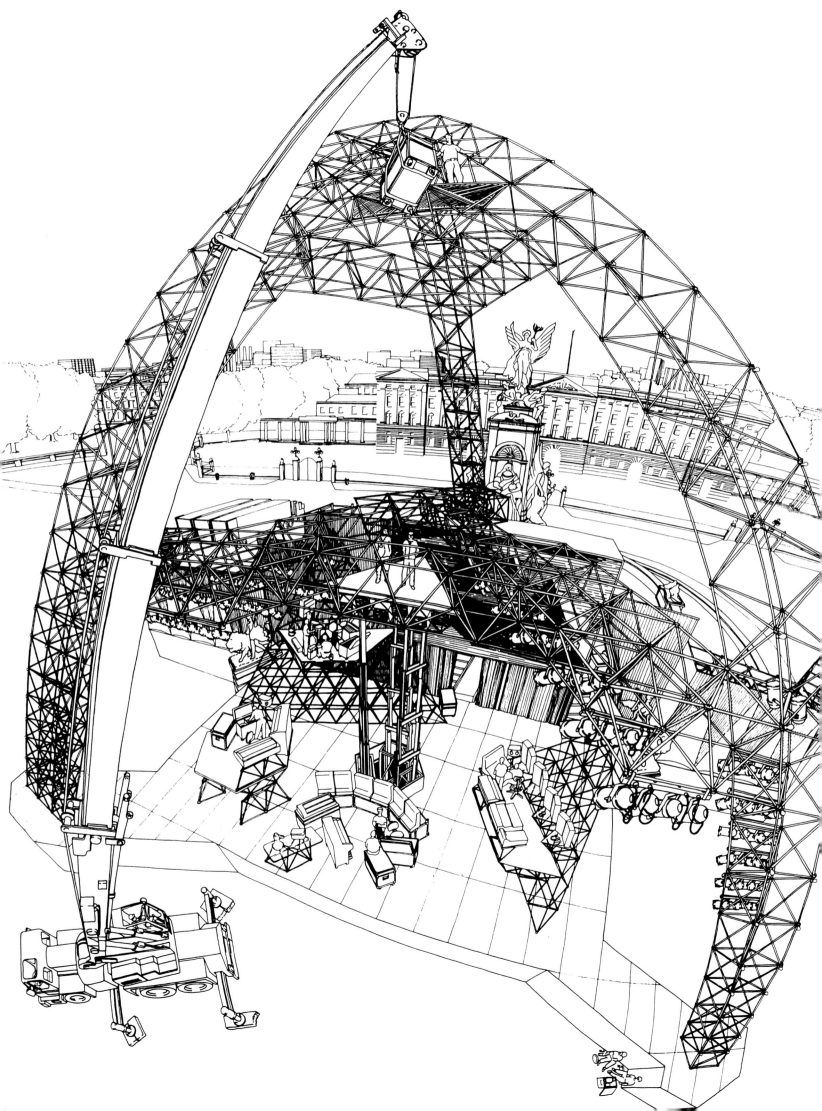

ROCK SETS

THE ASTONISHING ART OF ROCK CONCERT DESIGN
THE WORKS OF FISHER PARK

SUTHERLAND LYALL

with 184 illustrations, including 145 in colour

THAMES AND HUDSON

For Clea and Marcus

A fish-eye drawing of a Fisher Park set design for a proposed Jean-Michel Jarre concert outside Buckingham Palace in 1983 (*frontispiece*); the open pyramid was to have been recycled from the earlier *China* tour.

The demolition scene from *The Wall*, 1980–81 (*right*). This set for Pink Floyd represented a new level of architectural and engineering achievement in the designs of Fisher Park.

© 1992 Thames and Hudson Limited, London
Text © 1992 Sutherland Lyall

Typeset by Footnote Graphics, Warminster, Wilts
Printed and bound in Slovenia

Contents

Roger Waters' anti-authoritarian extravaganza *The Wall* (*right*) was staged on the Potzdamer Platz shortly after the demolition of the Berlin Wall in 1990. The show was created in two and a half months and it remains – in its one performance – the greatest example of Fisher Park's unique work in the fugitive architecture of rock sets.

Fisher Park drew on a number of sources for the Rolling Stones' *Steel Wheels* tour of 1989–90 (*below*) – existing steelworks and refineries, crossed with the imaginary urban structures of the novels of cyberpunk writer William Gibson and the menacing atmosphere of the movie *Blade Runner*.

The Rock Concert Designs of FISHER PARK

The Rolling Stones' *Steel Wheels* of 1989 and Roger Waters' *The Wall* in Berlin in 1990 are the two greatest, most spectacular rock concert designs ever devised. They were both the work of the London firm Fisher Park (architect Mark Fisher and engineer Jonathan Park) who were also responsible for the earlier 1980 Pink Floyd *The Wall*, whose size, complexity and audacity had set a standard for all subsequent rock shows.

In the world of rock, Fisher and Park are acknowledged as masters of the difficult scale and complexity of big stadium shows. They also get to work for the bands who can be persuaded to spend the kind of money which turns audiences' experience of watching a set of small figures performing a hundred yards away into a stunningly memorable occasion. What they do is to take the personality of the performers and reflect and reinforce them in as extreme a visual way as they will allow.

In the twelve months on either side of *Steel Wheels* and *The Wall*, they had designed Tina Turner's *foreign affair*, Janet Jackson's *Rhythm Nation 1814*, Whitney Houston's *I'm Your Baby Tonight*, the *Nelson Mandela International Tribute for a Free South Africa* and *Amitabh Bachchan in Concert* (both in Wembley Stadium), *Pavarotti in the Park* in London and *Guitar Legends* in Seville's Cartuja auditorium. They then worked on projects with Genesis, Simply Red, the Seville Expo, Bryan Adams, U2 and Mick Jagger. In other words, Fisher Park have operated from their formation at the very highest levels of design for the demanding world of rock music.

Fisher Park's set design (*right*) for *Guitar Legends*, Seville, 1991; the partnership was also commissioned to carry out project designs for the opening of the 1992 world fair in the same city.

A Moonrock event on Primrose Hill, London, 1971 (*opposite above*); the inflatable was designed by Jonathan Park and Graham Stevens.

The world's first solar balloon (*opposite below*) was designed by Dominic Michaelis and Jonathan Park in 1972.

Fisher Park's design for the Teacher puppet (*below*) for the film of *The Wall* in 1981 displays all their design ingenuity and attention to complex detail.

Unusually in the rock design world, Fisher and Park operate as a traditional architectural-engineering practice: the disciplines in which they were formally trained. Where other rock designers tend to produce only concept drawings which are worked up by others for building, Fisher and Park understand the nuts and bolts of their designs, because they have themselves drawn them out in the form of concept sketches, through mechanical engineering computer drawings, right down to the scaffolding layouts. They also know a lot about real-life technicalities, having served a hard apprenticeship as touring road crew on the American and European circuits.

What Fisher and Park do is to create instant high-performance, live architectural environments. Their palette of materials is aluminium, steel, scrim, cabling, projection cloth and fabric; their underlying structure is usually scaffolding. Their basic mechanical services are sound and lighting systems operating under sophisticated electronic control. They also include pyrotechnics launchers, video walls, cine and still projectors, lifts, cherry pickers, cranes and mobile generators. Their sites are a string of changing open spaces, sports stadiums and covered arenas. And, unlike any other architecture, theirs exists only when it is being used. It is arguably the only serious architectural manifestation of Pop.

Pop operates self-consciously in a commercial, cultural environment, in which the inner value of a thing depends on its current mass popularity. And that is precisely the way rock works. Bands are not interested in running a touring art business. The ultimate commercial function of set design is to add value to the price of a ticket. In a sense, the sets are distress purchases, essential only because of the need to augment and enhance the facilities at venues which are designed for a completely different activity – the in-the-round watching of major sporting events. Bands must operate in this kind of make-do venue because they are the only buildings with sufficient audience capacity to generate the big profits demanded by the stars. Fisher Park's rock architecture works or doesn't work according to the level of its popular appeal.

Unlike most architects, Fisher Park have no problem with the issue of style. They are not designing for their architectural peers and the architectural critics – who are rarely to be seen at rock concerts anyway – but for high-profile performers and their audiences. Style, therefore, is an essential element in their work. It provides the edge needed for rock to compete with the production values of the rival media of film and television; it provides the additional visual excitement in venues where the principal performers may only be seen by a tiny fraction of an immense audience; it provides a tangible identity for a closed and self-contained community during a given time-span.

Fisher Park – the Partnership

In 1964 Jonathan Park came to London with a Cambridge degree in mechanical sciences, the year before Mark Fisher started his first year at the Architectural Association School of Architecture. Park soon discovered London's new alternative culture, and he dived in head first as far as his daytime job as an engineer with Ove Arup and Partners and later Arup Associates allowed. In 1969 he became a part-time structures tutor at the Architectural Association and started working with the radical children's workshop, Moonrock, at the Roundhouse, the permanently crisis-ridden and immensely popular venue for the Underground in London's Camden Town.

Moonrock's manifesto was the destruction of 'the ghettoes of organized children's entertainment'. Every weekend two to four hundred children descended on the Roundhouse and other venues to get themselves involved with a riot of mixed-media activities: working with paint, make-up, film, music, theatre, inflatables and publications, and listening to fledgling rock bands such as Hawkwind, Curved Air and Ginger Johnson. The whole assembly would go to demonstrations, rock and arts festivals. It was a kind of semi-organized situationalist madness, where kids could do most of the things that their parents didn't want them to do, and certainly not at home.

At the end of 1970 Park formed a partnership with ex-Arup Associates architect Dominic Michaelis. For five years the two designed conversions, entered competitions and built two steel-and-glass houses, and the world's first working solar-powered balloon. By the middle of the decade Michaelis had moved completely into solar research and Park, now that the hippy culture had been overtaken by the bleak late-seventies ethos of Punk, went back to working as a freelance engineer and increased his commitment to the Architectural Association School of Architecture, where he took over the diploma technical studies department. In 1976, he found himself sharing an office with Mark Fisher.

In 1965 Fisher had come to London's Architectural Association for a seven-year course. He arrived in the middle of the Association's most creative and experimental period, when it energetically cultivated a whole range of contemporary radical architectural ideas and attitudes. The school encouraged its staff and its students to experiment, to discard the strait-jacket of the Modernist architectural establishment in order to discover new ways of looking at the purpose and function and scope of architecture.

Inflatables and Structures

During the sixties, inflatables figured large in the repertoire of avant-garde architectural students all over the world because they conformed to the criteria of indeterminacy, low weight and transience. More important, they could actually be *built*. Anybody with a roll of polythene, sticky tape and a vacuum cleaner could create large inflatable structures. Inflatables could be configured in many ways: as double-skin structures, as a group of cells, as interlinked arches – and the artist Christo produced several between 1966 and 1968 bound up with cabling. Less respectable among strict architectural circles (because they were insufficiently 'pure' structures) were the inflatable characters in the annual New York Macey's Thanksgiving Day parade in New York, and the various Disney theme parks.

Fisher had seen his first anthropomorphic inflatable *Mother of the Arts* in 1966. It was an inflatable woman designed by fellow Architectural Association students for the annual Lord Mayor's procession. It was based on Jean Tinguely's *She*, a long, hollow reclining woman whose vagina was the entrance to the exhibition inside shown earlier that year at Stockholm's Moderna Museet. In the procession, the designers of *Mother of the Arts* wielded coloured marker pens on the inner surface of the clear polythene blow-up.

Four years later Fisher and Simon Conolly built a 14-metre- (46-ft-) long inflatable submarine which toured on the back of a flatbed truck and featured at several exhibitions. In 1969 they had set up the firm, Air Structures Design, as a commercial vehicle for making lightweight tents and inflatables; the profits from this financed their student work on an inflatable mat which could be configured in a number of ways as a rigid structure. An interim version, *Automat*, was exhibited at the 1969 Paris Biennale and the two submitted a final version as their final year thesis project. *Dynamat* was a muti-celled inflatable structure which could be bent and shaped by varying the air pressure in each cell.

Inflatables research was going on around the world. A number of big corporations were experimenting with their possibilities and inflatables had joined the catalogue of approved alternative ways of building. In 1970, the American group Ant Farm produced *Inflatocookbook*, a collection of most of the available information on home-made inflatables. They also built a giant inflatable office for the production of the fourth issue of the *Whole Earth Catalog*, the compendium of materials, equipment and fittings for the alternative life style.

Jonathan Park, in his parallel event world, was working closely with London designer Graham Stevens on such things as inflatable water walks and bridges, domes and arcane inflatable forms for arts events.

Graduating in 1971, Fisher began to get small jobs designing inflatables for the theatre. He and Conolly designed parts of the *Jesus Christ Superstar* set and he subsequently worked on similar commissions for *The Rocky Horror Show* and with Piers Gough, one of the designers of *Mother of the Arts*, he designed the inflatable domes and pyrotechnics for John Boorman's movie *Zardoz*.

In 1973 he became a part-time tutor at the Architectural Association school where he set up the Nice Ideas Unit, an ironic title which referred to the fact that most of the school's other work was done on paper. The intention of the unit was to learn about the principles of architecture by *building* projects.

Domes and inflatables were not the only lightweight structures favoured by architecture students. A great deal of theoretical research into membranes and work on shell and tension structures was also being done by such engineers as Frei Otto in Germany and Ted Happold at Arup's in Britain. A number of young architects and tutors were also testing out newly developed structural theories and systems, building structures from cheap, readily available materials. One of the Nice Ideas Unit's early projects was a stretched-cable climbing net designed and built by the students for a children's playground in north London. It was designed as a model and built to adopt a stable predetermined shape when it was erected on site.

At the Architectural Association, one of Park's groups built a bamboo lattice shell over a rooftop patio at the school's building in Bedford Square. Made from bamboo poles lashed in a lattice, the original design was developed from an upside-down model in which all the forces were in tension. The beauty of this structure was that, turned right side up and built full-size in bamboo to form a domed shape, all the forces in the members were in compression and thus stable. His group later added a fabric canopy, designed using the same modelling method. The whole structure lasted eighteen months, after which the bamboo started to rot.

That year Fisher began teaching in the diploma school and shared an office with Park. They also shared their curiosity about advanced structures and, although Park better understood the heavy mathematics and Fisher the aesthetics, they had a common interest in building them. Park had built many inflatables during his Moonrock years, while Fisher was earning money from making commercial inflatables and continuing his experiments with mobile pneumatic structures.

They were not working in isolation, however. In the parallel worlds of alternative theatre, happenings, performance art and music, much theoretical importance was placed on transience, ad-hocness, spontaneity and use of settings which had been assembled from found objects. In architecture, tutors and students at many schools around the world were conducting similar experiments with cheap materials. In Italy, especially, a number of design groups were addressing themselves to defining the new city in terms of discontinuity and mobility – the all-embracing No Stop City.

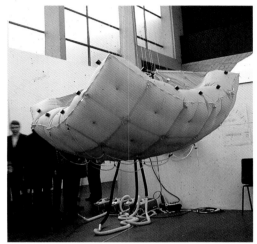

Simon Conolly's and Mark Fisher's inflatable submarine (*far left above*) was used in a procession and as a static unit at several exhibitions in 1970.

Mother of the Arts (1966) (*top*); this inflatable was designed and built by Piers Gough and other Architectural Association students for the annual Lord Mayor's procession.

Fisher's and Conolly's final year Architectural Association project, *Dynamat* (*left above*), was a multi-celled structure which could be transported folded in, say, the boot of a car, and then inflated into whatever shape was needed at the time.

The Architectural Association Nice Ideas Unit *Playnet* (*above*) was constructed for a north London adventure playground in 1971.

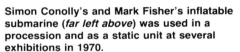

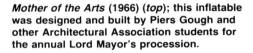

Mark Fisher and Piers Gough designed the inflatables for the set of John Boorman's film *Zardoz* (*far left*).

Jonathan Park with Architectural Association students designed this bamboo lattice structure with stressed fabric canopy over a terrace at the school (*left centre*).

An inflatable project designed by Chrysalis in California; this group was a strong early influence on Fisher Park.

Influences – Archigram and Temporary Architecture

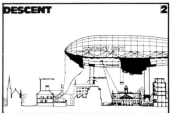
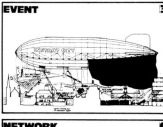
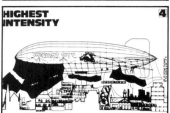
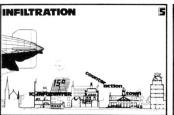

One of the generally accepted new wisdoms was that somewhere and somehow a major key to the new architecture was technology. It was a time when astronauts were soon to walk on the moon, yet architects still designed buildings according to a primitive craft technology developed by the ancient Babylonians. So the new technology and the new consumer durable gadgetry being developed in the United States seemed to offer architecture limitless horizons. Under the influence of Buckminster Fuller, the American polymath and proselytizer of lightweight, portable structures, the sixties avant-garde became preoccupied with the idea of indeterminacy, transience and the belief that architecture was very much less to do with what a structure looked like than with what it offered its users in terms of a controllable environment.

The protagonists of this position in Britain and eventually around the world were the Archigram group. Their two gurus were the architect Cedric Price and the architectural critic Reyner Banham, one of the fathers of Pop.

Archigram's influence spread around the world, partly because of the brilliance of the group's design and drawing and partly because its members were prepared to go all the way in exploring strands of thinking and pursuing the possibilities of new and nearly-available technology. The central principle of the group was the pursuit of a pleasanter life, one which was easier, full of possibilities and susceptible to change via the manipulation of the immediate environment as needs, desires and the state of technology changed. They were interested in the idea of architecture as an indeterminate thing, instantly creatable, transient, ephemeral, expendable, responsive, interactive and capable of regular modification as the people who used it found their needs changing.

Archigram's designs tended to be lightweight, mechanistic in the sense of celebrating the intrinsic design qualities of found industrial objects and *assembled* from a catholic collection of structures, nets, tents, inflatables, industrial equipment, cranes, trucks, pylons, Portakabins, dot matrix and television screens, portable staging – a kit of parts.

This kit-of-parts idea was enshrined in Archigram's notion of the Plug-in-City, a series of basic structures into which individual living units could be plugged until the inhabitant decided to take his dwelling somewhere else. One of their most widely admired concepts was Instant City, a

travelling kit of parts which would transform a local town or suburb for a short period and then move on, leaving some of its elements as incitements to the local people to begin the transformation of their own environment.

Archigram's work had close parallels in the work of contemporary artists such as Christo, whose temporary wrapping of objects, particularly buildings, subscribed to the notion of transience, of art with an ephemeral existence which squared roughly with the group's own emphasis on non-permanent architecture. This bricolaging Dadaist style, this putting *found* elements together was a major characteristic of the contemporary work of Jean Tinguely. His enigmatic kinetic and auto-destruct art struck other chords because of its movement and because it was invariably constructed from *found* industrial objects welded, motorized and bolted together in an apparently *ad hoc* manner.

The Archigram group was not particularly worried about building real buildings, though for people of Fisher's circle, a generation younger than the Archigram group, this was unsatisfactory. For them architecture was to do with three-dimensional, practical reality, with *making* buildings. Ironically Archigram, which had revolted against the smug certainties of post-war Modernist architects, found their own positions being dismissed by a second wave of young architects who, while they remained subscribers to the fundamental Archigram positions, nevertheless found sustenance in Fuller, who had turned his paper exercises into real buildings.

One of Archigram's sequences of illustrations for the Instant City (*top*), an airship-based travelling kit of parts for temporarily transforming localities with entertainments and events before moving on to the next location; it was intended to incite the indigenous population to take their environment into their own hands – a kind of imagination pump-priming operation.

The Skylon at the 1951 Festival of Britain (*far left*) is remembered by Jonathan Park as another early influence.

Haus Rucker Co built Oasis no 7 (*left*) at the 1972 Documenta at Kassel. It embodied many of the ideas of Archigram, creating a slick modern environment plugged into an existing building.

The super-spectacular rock shows of the eighties and nineties look like a major new phenomenon. But their logistics, spectacle and, up to a point, intentions belong to an older tradition. The great American travelling circuses of the nineteenth and early twentieth century developed from a train of mule- and horse-drawn wagons to 120-rail-car circuses shifting 16,000-seater big tops, cages, equipment, animals and road crew across the continent on the backs of flatbed railway trucks. In the fifties, with the advent of television and the gradual decline of the travelling circus, the Ringling Brothers and Barnum & Bailey outfits changed from rail to road and started setting up in stadiums – less than fifteen years before the Beatles played Shea Stadium. The circus was a peripatetic big business. At a technical level it had worked out solutions to the problems of creating instant, transient environments many years before rock'n'roll.

A link between the two eras was the touring rockabilly show, the Louisiana Hoedown, Colonel Parker's shipping of Elvis Presley around small Southern stadiums where he played from the back of a flatbed trailer with early primitive amplification. In the thirties Parker had worked as a carny for The Royal American Shows started by Carl Sedelmyer, whose 70-car trains of crew Pullmans, flatcars and a neon tube factory travelled the American rail network into every remote rural district. The means of transport may have changed for the modern rock tour, but the scale of the operation can be comparable to that of the great circuses, especially where top bands, such as the Rolling Stones and Pink Floyd, are concerned.

Influences – the Road Show

Showman's hype perhaps (there are rather more than 100 railway cars here) (*below*), but this Ringling Bros poster of the turn-of-the-century gives some idea of the complexity of scale and organization involved in touring the great circuses around the United States.

Colonel Parker, for much debated reasons, toured Elvis Presley around small Southern stadiums with a rudimentary sound system and no set (*right*).

Stadium Rock – the Early Years

The rock stadium touring industry is twenty-seven years old. It began in 1965 when the Beatles sang outdoors at Shea Stadium, New York, on flat staging above the pitcher's mound, with a rudimentary sound system completely defeated by the non-stop shriek of 45,000 teenage fans. As stadiums and stadium rock shows got bigger, rock itself began to lose its early quality of direct, dirty, raw emotion. Rock critic Robert Sandall has pointed out that the cost of a concert ticket used to be half the price of a vinyl album: 'Then it was an emblematic thing, a meeting on behalf of the youth party, a communal event. What was happening on stage was almost incidental: as spectacle they didn't really have much to offer.'

However regretful people from the sixties may be about the fading away of discussions about the future of rock 'n' roll, present-day rock shows are a simple response to the commercialized, cleaned-up-for-radio nature of rock music, and to the heterogeneous nature of contemporary audiences, which these days include a heavy sprinkling of approving parents.

People now go to rock shows for many reasons. One of them is to be in the same place as the group, in the same way that the faithful visit the tents of charismatic preachers to acquire something of their numinosity by occupying the same ritual space. Another is the rare pleasure of having fun on a day out with a crowd of 60,000 people and hearing good music very loud. But their notions of spectacle have been made more sophisticated by movies and television, their expectations of facilities by other public events such as major sports meetings. And their expectations of sound quality have been raised by CD recordings. The fact is that in outdoor venues the acoustic and atmospheric environment is idiosyncratic. Even the most accomplished sound director does not expect a live performance in a stadium to sound the same as a recording. That of course begs the old question of the relative authenticity of loud live music as against that of recorded performances.

In addition there is the problem, only partly answered by big relay video screens around the stadium, of giving two-thirds of the audience some idea of what the

The Beatles playing at Shea Stadium, New York, 1965, the first major outdoor rock'n'roll stadium show (*opposite above and below*).

The 1969 Woodstock and the 1970 Isle of Wight festivals were legendary outdoor events for American and British rock aficionados (*top and above*).

The set at the 1978 Knebworth festival had a stressed fabric skin roof (*below left*). The Electric Light Orchestra at Toronto, 1978 (*below centre*): the flying saucer rose up at the beginning of the show. The Rolling Stones set at Leeds 1982 (*below right*) was notable for its Yamazaki-designed profiled scrims.

performers at the other end of the stadium are actually doing. As early as the mid seventies Mick Jagger was saying to one of his touring crew, Brian Croft, that the people at the back of a stadium could not possibly see the tiny figures on stage. For the Rolling Stones' concert at Knebworth in 1976, back-projected video relay screens were installed half-way up the hill.

The crude answer is to make the set big and interesting, and to have other things going on around it. As bands such as Queen, the Rolling Stones and Pink Floyd had grasped, it was necessary to make a big statement with a big structure. So, bands accept the notion that spectacular sets, lighting and pyrotechnics enhance their rapport with the audience, and spectacle has become a critical factor in the successful presentation of stadium rock shows for the bands that can afford it.

In the late sixties there had been a series of very big rock festivals, such as Woodstock in the United States and the Isle of Wight shows in England, which were attended by hundreds of thousands of people. These were tribal events of the new counterculture in which the act of participation, sleeping overnight, smoking dope, practising friendliness and sex and listening to the succession of bands were all more or less equally important. Occasionally the sets were more than makeshift scaffolding stages, such as the polythene-covered pyramid which made its appearance at the Glastonbury festival in 1972. With the burning out of the hippy movement in the early seventies, there was no longer the cultural impetus to sustain such large congregations.

In the mid seventies, when Fisher and Park worked their first shows as special effects crew with Pink Floyd's American *Animals* tour, most rock tours were still rudimentary affairs, with the band on a 6-metre-by-12-metre (20-ft-by-40-ft) stage with a roof overhead supporting lighting trusses and the PA – the two stacks of loudspeakers – either side of the stage. With the exception of very popular performers, it was not until the late seventies that bands had enough cash to build their visions in fully worked-out form.

The touring shows of the sixties and early seventies were gruelling, primitive, not necessarily profitable and often done as a promotional back-up to the group's latest album or single. The difference between them and the tours of the late eighties and nineties is a matter partly of scale and partly of sheer professionalism, although many of the personnel are the same. Those who have managed to survive some years of the extreme tour-side stress of drugs, sex and rock, hard physical labour and the constant, gut-gnawing anticipation of major equipment failure, tend to come out of it case-hardened and very competent at what they do. So, too, the sound and lighting equipment has become extremely sophisticated and consumes vast amounts of power.

The other big difference is the amount of money involved and the fact that the tours are now expected to make serious profits. Big tours today involve tens, occasionally hundreds of millions of dollars. From one point of view they should be seen as peripatetic corporations – managing pre-arranged sales on site and dealing in the sort of money that medium- to large-sized commercial enterprises turn over every year – but all run from hotel rooms with calculators, telephones, faxes and laptop computers.

PINK FLOYD
ANIMALS

TOUR 1977

One of pyrotechnician Wilf Scott's jobs was to fire sheep from mortars at the back of the set over the stage to float down into the audience during the number 'Sheep'. The sheep were made from tea-bag paper, with holes in the feet to provide a parachute effect and weighted to keep them upright. For each show half a dozen were fired one by one during the song.

On several dates it had not been possible to fire the sheep and Scott had too many on his hands. Fed up, at Chicago he decided to fire off all the spares as well. The band was not amused when salvoes of sheep kept floating overhead into the audience long into the next number, 'Pigs on the Wing, Part 2'.

The effectiveness of the sheep as a dramatic adjunct to the show can be gauged from this photograph of a trial firing (*below*).

Fisher and Park's introduction to rock was in designing and touring a set of inflatables with Pink Floyd's American *Animals* tour of 1977. During a December 1976 photocall for the *Animals* album cover, Pink Floyd's giant inflatable pig had escaped from its moorings at Battersea power station. Designed by Jeffrey Shaw of Amsterdam-based Eventstructure Research Group, it had been constructed by Ballon Fabrik in Germany. The ring connecting the mooring cable to the loom of cables attached to the pig snapped, and the pig ascended majestically through the Heathrow flight path and landed later in Kent. Pink Floyd wanted to include additional inflatables for the American leg of the tour and asked Aubrey Powell to find a new inflatables designer. Powell was a member of Hipgnosis, the graphic designers responsible for the album cover. He contacted Andrew Sanders, an art director with experience of waxwork figures. Uncertain where to begin, Sanders contacted the doorman at the Palace Theatre in London, the unofficial *Yellow Pages* for specialist theatre skills. Two years previously the doorman had taken down Fisher's details after he had worked on some inflatable props for a Barry Humphries show. The link was established with the Pink Floyd production team.

The new set of inflatables represented a nuclear family. Made up of a businessman, his blowsy wife on a sofa, a son, daughter and half a child, it was an ironic reference to the official statistic that the average British nuclear family had 2.5 offspring. Associated with these anthropomorphic figures were typical consumer durables: a television set, a refrigerator and a full-sized Cadillac – and the standard reference of the time to police and authority, the giant pig.

Pink Floyd asked Sanders and Fisher to create the family of new inflatables together with their control mechanisms. Fisher asked Park to collaborate on engineering their rigging and controls – and tour the show from Miami to Montreal for six months.

Roger Waters wanted the figures to be life-size, but Fisher thought they should relate to the scale of an auditorium. Although they reached a compromise of three times life-size, he was still unhappy. The rescued helium-filled pig was used for publicity, and new show pigs made were from its patterns.

Sanders and Fisher sculpted the scale models for the inflatables in styrofoam and, using an overhead projector, enlarged tissue paper patterns from them up to full-size cutting patterns. Rob Harries, ex-Hornsey College of Art student and a member of the British pneumatics circuit, sewed the figures ready for installation and inflation with industrial fans. Park engineered the rigging and designed and built the raising and lowering systems for the inflatables.

Pink Floyd – the Beginnings

In the mid sixties three of Pink Floyd – Roger Waters, Rick Wright and Nick Mason – had been at the Regent Street Polytechnic School of Architecture and Syd Barrett at Camberwell School of Art. More or less contemporaries of Fisher and Park, they had come from the same sixties radical design background.

The band went professional in 1967, after building up a following in the Underground, especially at the UFO Club and Middle Earth. Almost from the beginning, their performances were unlike any others. Their numbers went on for half an hour and they played while being washed by images from projectors, moving oil wheels, ether-injected slides, movie films and whatever strange visual effects the developing technology of acid culture could produce. Within a couple of years their shows had become legendary, intensely visual live performance art. Their music, with its unrelenting, gut-vibrating, low-frequency notes, its collaging of sounds from *found* sources and the extraordinary and lengthy development of single chords, was right at the sharp end of the new wave, as close as it was possible to get to the dream-like, free-form, hallucinatory ethos and imagery of psychedelia.

The *Animals* tour was especially notable for its use of inflatables: the Father figure (*above*) and the Pig (*right*) before its escape.

The tour carried a stock of explodable pigs. In the dark backstage, his hair standing on end from the static charge, Fisher would fill a pig with propane and helium, alert the line of crew men holding the mooring rope behind the stage, let it fly up more than 100 metres (330 ft) and press the ignition button. In Milwaukee, Fisher and winch boss Richard Hartman decided to experiment with a mixture of acetylene and oxygen instead of propane. The band had been given a special injunction to keep the noise down because of the proximity of a veterans' hospital. Fisher sent up the pig with the new mixture inside it and pressed the button. There was a huge flash and the pig disappeared (*far right*). A split second later they heard on enormous detonation in the night sky. The cable crew went down like dominoes, showered with confetti. The band was badly shocked.

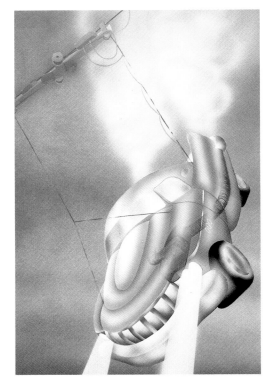

The American *Animals* set was designed to be located across one end of an outdoor stadium, with the PA stacked in towers either side of the stage and a main backdrop formed by the big circular projection screen Pink Floyd had used on several previous tours. Lighting was suspended from pneumatic telescopic towers either side of the stage, from cherry pickers on front of the stage and from lights fixed around the perimeter of the circular screen. The inflatables travelled along a very long cable stretching over the stage from right to left held up at each end by mobile hydraulic cranes. Another long cable, sometimes as long as 400 metres (1300 ft) depending on the stadium, stretched from the back of the venue to behind the set attached to the stadium structure or by additional cranes. It carried the pig.

For the pig's number it emerged above the audience, flew overhead along the long cable, stopping here and there to snort at the audience, and finally disappeared behind the set. A few seconds later it reappeared to float up into the night sky and suddenly explode. The second pig was in reality a disposable version filled with helium, with an inner bag of propane fitted with an igniter.

The inflatables were packed unobtrusively in boxes to the sides of the set. On cue, built-in industrial fans rapidly inflated them and they were then hauled up overhead by winches suspended from the long cross-stage cable. The Father was slung from a travelling winch which flew him over the stage where he slowly descended into a crumpled heap during the final verse of his song.

From the Pyramid to the Gantry

Half-way through their 1975 American tour, Pink Floyd decided they wanted a pyramid to decorate their stage set. They got one built in a great rush, during a four-week break in the middle of the tour. It stood 20 metres (66 ft) square, and 20 metres high. During the show, the top section of the pyramid was to detach itself and float away: the flying pyramid of the United States dollar banknote and masonic cults.

It was constructed from a fabric-covered inflatable frame lifted by a helium balloon inside. On its maiden flight on a windy June evening in Pittsburg the structure tilted sideways, allowing the unsecured balloon to escape through the open bottom. The pyramid fell out of the sky, writing off several cars in the stadium car park and the idea was temporarily shelved.

Pink Floyd owned Britannia Row, a company which was responsible for all its production work. After the 1977 tour, Graeme Fleming, Britannia Row's production director, hired Fisher and Park to resurrect the pyramid. Park designed the steelwork in the form of a 20-metre- (66-ft-) high cube of lightweight lattice girders with sloping guy ropes at each corner forming the outline of a truncated pyramid. Fisher, who was living in Canada at the time, designed the upper pyramid. He made a number of models and built full-sized mockups of the corners.

When the steelwork was completed, Pink Floyd decided to abandon the pyramid project. Fisher and Park saw it as an ideal opportunity to put the theoretical notions of transient structures to the test.

They re-configured the structure as a portable staging gantry to be erected by two mobile cranes and a very small crew. They added a lightweight fabric roof and produced a series of drawings showing its possible uses. It eventually paid for itself when it was transported on two flatbed trucks to form the stage for, among others, Led Zeppelin at Knebworth, Queen at Saarbrucken and in Nuremberg. Later Britannia Row extended it in anticipation of another performance of *The Wall*. But it spent most of the time overgrown with nettles at Knebworth and was last seen on the edge of an airfield in Toronto, where in 1988 Pink Floyd had intended to use it in a cut-down form.

The rock production world had viewed the gantry with suspicion. Its biggest problem was that two cranes were needed to erect it. The construction industry rents cranes all over the world, but not all stadiums have access doors big enough to take them, and the rock touring world was uneasy about heavy equipment which required specialist operatives. But engineers liked it: the Britannia Row Gantry won a British Steel award for innovative structures in 1979.

However spectacular the use to which the gantry was put, it had become clear to Fisher Park that scaffolding was an inextricable part of their design constraints. Scaffolding made more sense on the road. It had none of the design qualities of systems worked out by several decades of architects and engineers and its jointing was crude. But crews were familiar with it, it could be used in practically any configuration, it went up quickly and it could be hired anywhere in the Western world. Yet, in spite of the relative limitations of available materials and their occasional crudeness, Fisher Park have still managed to create some very impressive architectural structures. But there lies their peculiar genius.

The *Animals'* Cadillac as it was designed (*opposite left top*) and finally built (*opposite left centre*).

This massive pyrotechnic display signalled the end of the *Animals* show (*opposite left below*).

Rehearsing the *Animals* inflatables before one of the 1977 shows (*above*); they were stored in boxes at the side of the stage before being rapidly inflated and winched up and into position. It was this show which first enabled both Fisher and Park to give massive expression to their work on the development of inflatables during the nineteen-seventies.

Fisher's and Park's design for the new Britannia Row flying pyramid detached from the base and guided by long cables (*left*).

One of the 1978 Fisher proposals for the way the gantry could be used by other groups (*above*).

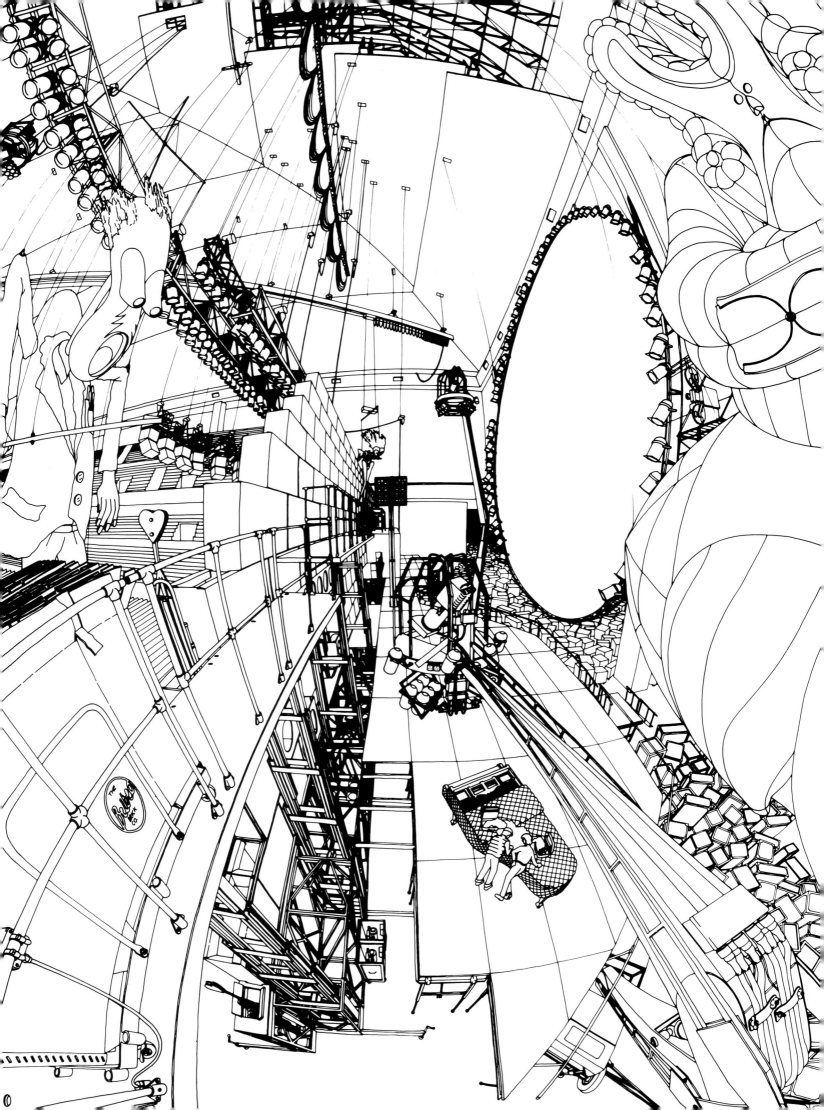

PINK FLOYD

THE WALL

WORLD TOUR 1980–81

Mark Fisher's 1980 fish-eye drawing of the rear of The Wall set (opposite).

Building the wall in performance (above).

The beginning of the second half of the show; Roger Waters can be seen on a fold-out section of the wall (below).

At the very end of the last performance of *Animals* in July 1978 Roger Waters spat contemptuously over the rioting front rows of the Montreal audience. He had flipped, severely stressed out by a long tour during which he had become increasingly depressed by the impossibility of establishing any musical relationship with huge stadium audiences. By the end of the year he had enlisted Mark Fisher and the brilliantly scabrous cartoonist Gerald Scarfe to work on the design of his new show. Its theme was the alienation of the rock star from his audience, symbolized by the building of a wall right across the stage.

Unlike most rock concert programmes (which were and still are a judicious mix of new songs and old favourites), *The Wall* was more akin to an opera. Rock critics of the performances, by then hardened on early Punk, found it trivial. Audiences may not have understood the story-line, but at least they picked up on the general theme of alienation and rebellion. Nevertheless, the existence of a plot gave internal purpose and meaning to the series of spectacular special effects.

As finally developed, *The Wall*'s plot was about a pop star called Pink, who recalls his childhood: father killed in the war, over-protective mother, school, teachers, pop stardom, his distant wife's infidelity and, with the laying of the last brick, alienation. The band played behind the wall for much of the second half, a nightmare sequence involving a fascist rally, followed by a court scene in which Pink was denounced by all the characters who had persecuted him – followed by a kind of redemption with the demolition of the wall.

Various sections of this urban psychodrama were underlined with special effects. As the show opened, the Father's death was relived by an aircraft swooping over the audience's heads and crashing in flames into the top of the wall. In the fifth song, 'Another Brick in the Wall, Part 2', a 15-metre (49-ft) puppet of a schoolmaster menaced across the forestage – at which time stagehands start building the wall. In the song 'Mother' an inflatable Mother ascended from behind the wall and at one moment a large section of inflatable wall burst from her arm. The Wife rose over the wall during the hotel room song, 'Don't Leave Me Now', to dangle malevolently. In the fascist fantasy sequence a giant pig broke through the top of the completed wall and travelled deep into the auditorium where it snorted and threatened the audience below before turning around and retreating behind the wall. The familiar circular Pink Floyd screen was back-projected with images, including Scarfe's 'Fucking Flowers' animation. During the second half the wall itself was used as a projection screen for Scarfe's animations of the rally and trial scenes.

Fisher and Park designed the puppets for the show, including the Teacher, here menacing Roger Waters (*above*), and the Wife (*opposite below left*). They also developed five 6-metre-(20-ft-) long wall-builders' platforms on hydraulic lifts which rose up as each course was laid (*below*). The cardboard bricks were stabilized by dropping every second one over a telescopic mast fixed along the baseline of the wall. The masts extended further upwards as each course of bricks was laid. At the top of the telescopic masts were heart-shaped levers: the knockers. To collapse the wall the columns retracted under power with the knockers thrashing back and forward, knocking the bricks down course by course from the top. The ten telescopic columns with their heart mechanisms were custom-made, but they and the lifts were based on standard devices used in rock shows for lifting heavy lighting gear. They were extensively modified by Park in Seattle to work from a much more powerful and controllable hydraulic power source, and they were built into their own modular dollies, which became part of the stage. The platforms were made from honeycomb aluminium panels from a surplus store. All the aluminium work was done in local fabrication shops.

Initially, Fisher produced a series of storyboards explaining to the band how the show could work and look. They had started the slow process of recording the album in April, but it was not until September, still recording, that they agreed to tour with the Waters–Scarfe–Fisher show concept.

When the band gave the go-ahead, Fisher regrouped with Park to sort out the technicalities of making the idea work as a touring live performance. Their function was to design and supervise the making and building of the set – everything except sound and lighting – and then tour with it. Scarfe was heavily involved with an army of animators for the cine projections and with Fisher in translating his sketches into large-scale, three-dimensional inflatables. Fisher and Park were finalizing the method of constructing and demolishing the wall. With their backgrounds, they inevitably focused on creating mechanisms which were as minimal and structurally elegant as possible; they had to be light and modular, so that they were manhandlable and could be packed with the greatest economy on the backs of trucks on tour.

All the components were shipped to a sound stage at Culver City and the assembling of the set was begun. Fisher Park's first discovery was that they had toleranced everything too precisely. Their second discovery was that prototypes need time to be tested out, especially when the people having to operate them are battered by noise and flashing lights. On delivery, the hydraulic motors for the lifts failed to work properly. After a week immersed in hydraulic fluid, trying to redefine the laws of physics, the crew discovered that the factory had incorrectly set the electric motors for the pumps.

Pink Floyd tour manager Graeme Fleming decided to test out how easily the show could be moved from one venue to another and ordered a series of load-ins and load-outs between Culver City and the Los Angeles Arena. The band's manager Steve O'Rourke, who had not yet seen the set, came into the Arena where it had been set up in twenty-four hours and said, 'Cor, fuck. Is that what it's really like?' Fisher and Park decided that everything they did thereafter would have to have a 'Cor, Fuck' factor.

The designers soon grasped that, however well conceived the mechanical design, it had to be operated under anarchic and unexpected conditions. The classic rock term is 'winging it'.

Although *The Wall* was designed to travel, it played a total of only twenty-nine shows, five in the Los Angeles Arena, five at Nassau Coliseum, Long Island, and the other nineteen dates at Earls Court, London and the Westfalenhalle, Dortmund. A year later the show was staged again before a live audience for the filming of *The Wall* movie. That footage never appeared in the film.

The primary technical problem was how to build the wall across an arena during the performance. The 80-metre-by-10-metre (260-ft-by-33-ft) wall, laid in English garden bond, had to be built from behind to avoid having stagehands and scaffolding or lifts distracting the audience. For the same reason, there could not be any scaffolding at the back: the wall had to appear to tumble down, leaving a clear space behind it. The bricks had to be lightweight and transportable in large numbers. After trying out a variety of possibilities, Fisher and Park decided on cardboard boxes with a diaphragm across the middle. Made in the UK by a cardboard box manufacturer, they could be folded flat and shipped around in thousands on mobile pallets, whose tubular aluminium side frames could be removed to form the safety railings for the bricklayer's platforms. The photograph (*opposite*) shows the set prepared for the beginning of the performance.

The inflatable pig (*right*) was flown and manipulated from a 40-metre- (130-ft-) long aluminium track, devised by *Animals* rigger Rocky Paulson, and suspended from the roof. The pig could be raised, lowered and panned on its journey through the top of the wall over the audience and back. Fisher tested the system by riding on the back of the pig.

An Inflatable Venue – 'The Slug'

More than a year before the tour, in late 1978, Fisher had worked on plans for the construction of the wall and on studies for *The Slug* (*below*). If the theme of *The Wall* was alienation, it made a kind of sense to stage the shows in alienated environments, such as ugly, derelict city fringe sites or wastelands, or to create an alien environment in the countryside. *The Slug* was a 100-metre- (330-ft-) long inflatable venue which could be delivered flat, blown up and supplied with services from container trucks parked inside. The show could go on – and then move, packed up in trucks, to the next venue. It was eventually abandoned because of the problems of licensing temporary wasteland sites, which Fisher and Park were to experience again with the Jean-Michel Jarre *Docklands* show.

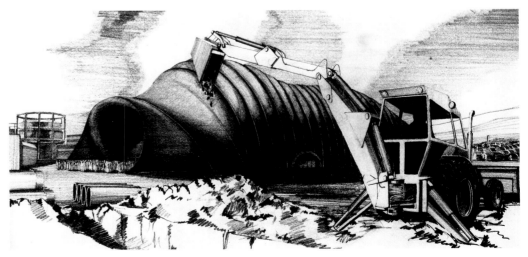

Beyond *The Wall* – the Development of Fisher Park

Following *The Wall*, Fisher and Park designed the set for a Stevie Wonder show and Fisher went with it as a tour carpenter. Park went back to working independently, regularly coming in to engineer Fisher's design projects. There were few engineers about with Park's unusual eye for solutions to ostensibly crazy projects. The two were to work this way on Jean-Michel Jarre's *China* tour, the big articulated Teacher puppet for the film of *The Wall*, the 1982 Ultravox *Quartet* tour and the Hippodrome nightclub for which they designed an intensely complicated lighting system. They worked together on the Hippodrome for nearly a year and decided in 1984 to formalize the partnership.

Over the next six years they designed a number of projects for Jean-Michel Jarre, Tina Turner, Roger Waters, Barry Manilow, Murray Head, Wham! and George Michael, George Lam, the Rolling Stones and a number of other performers, not all of whom could find backing for their proposals.

Fisher has remained primarily a designer, while Park has increasingly moved away from detailed structural and mechanical engineering to the broad choreography of shows and their conception. This arrangement involves tensions. Yet, as individuals, they find the best way of working is in taking adversarial design roles.

Animals, *The Wall* and other shows which Fisher and Park toured provided them with a hard apprenticeship in the realities of touring: the fate of impractical bits of scenery and sets that needed to be designed to last the rigours of being erected and dismantled five times a week for months on end.

In the big-league rock'n'roll world, Fisher and Park found themselves inducted into a team ethos in which the star is the client and the performance director because he or she has written most of the songs and has a very clear idea about what the show should say. In the early years, it was often creatively difficult. The bands had rather mundane conceptions of sets and were more interested in the gimmicks devised by the lighting designer who always had the ear of the band on the road. Fisher and Park, however, had the good fortune of working with the only major band which understood the multi-dimensional possibilities of a performance. Pink Floyd had changed them from a pair of interesting designers into a focused operation. From their point of view, it was a happy accident that they were creating architectonic structures for a group whose design background coincided with their own and in particular for Roger Waters, who took great design risks.

Jonathan Park on the right and Mark Fisher on the left (*below*).

The drawing at the foot of the page shows the major elements of *The Wall*: the Pig hanging from its track, the aeroplane on its path to crash through the top of the wall.

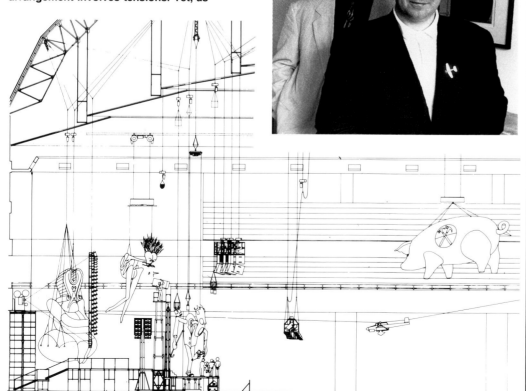

STEVIE WONDER

HOTTER THAN JULY

1980

This view of the *Hotter than July* set is from the rear of the Wembley Arena auditorium.

The green shade netting, originally developed for use in the Middle East desert, takes on a new quality as the enclosure for Stevie Wonder's set (*opposite below*).

After *Animals* Fisher and Park were regularly commissioned by Britannia Row to design productions for other rock bands. Later in 1980 they designed the set for Stevie Wonder's *Hotter than July* tour. Fisher toured with the show as carpenter. Stretched over the stage was a membrane roof made from shade netting – a fabric designed in Germany in the seventies for temporary shade over large areas. The high points in the roof were supported by broad plywood blades forming umbrellas, to avoid tearing the cloth. The umbrellas were fixed to the tops of the hydraulic man-lift columns recycled from *The Wall*. The ingenious combination of *ad hoc* architecture and engineering with a regard for overall design was already beginning to show itself.

Fisher's design for the *Hotter than July* set; the tensioned shade netting forms a fabric-engineering style structure (*below*).

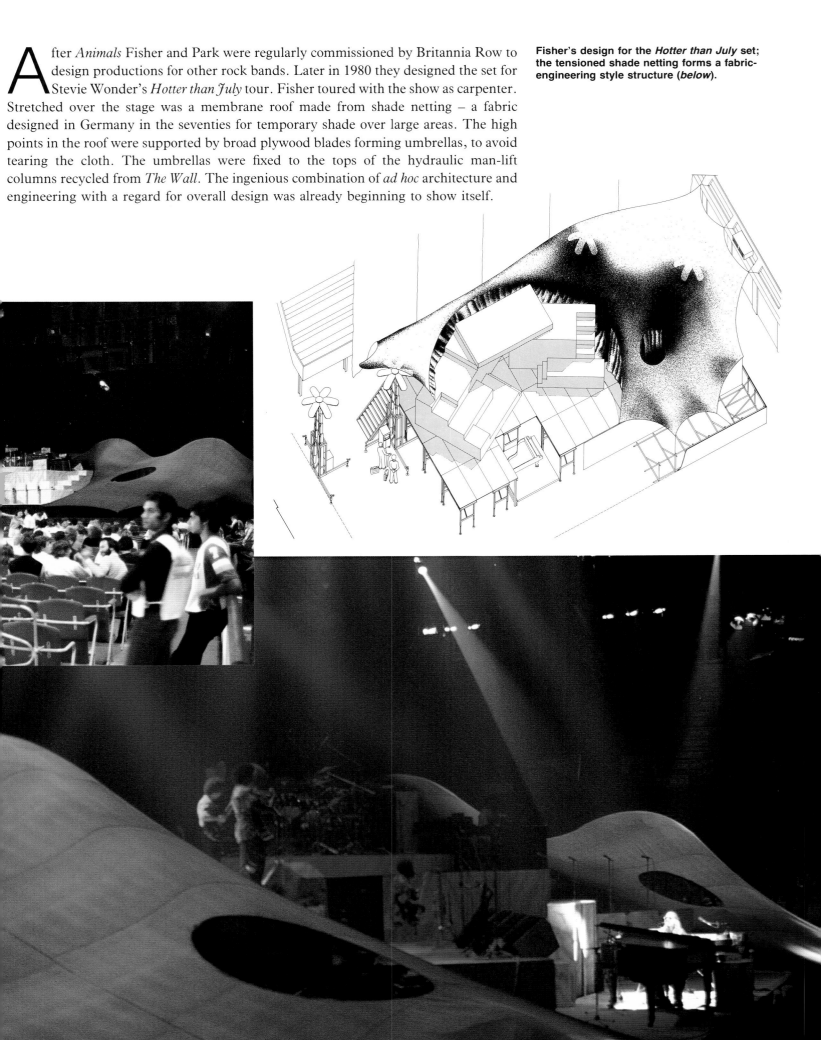

JEAN-MICHEL JARRE
THE CONCERTS IN CHINA

TOUR 1981

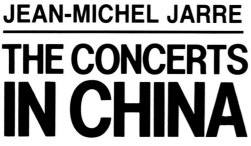

Early in 1981, Jean-Michel Jarre contacted Britannia Row about doing a show for him. Fisher produced a quick pitch, and went to see Jarre in Paris. Jarre then went to see one of the performances of *The Wall* which Fisher and Park were working on in Dortmund. There Fisher showed him a series of sketches for a show in Peking's Forbidden City; Jarre so liked the idea that he took Fisher with him to China the following month to negotiate with the authorities and reconnoitre venues. Jarre had been negotiating for several years with the Chinese authorities to stage the first heavy rock show in a China which was still closed in the aftermath of the Cultural Revolution. By April Fisher had taken over the job and worked out a variety of schemes, bringing in Park to work on the engineering. In July Jarre and Fisher went again to China to present the designs for outdoor venues. These were later to be changed to indoor venues in Peking and Shanghai.

In Peking Fisher and Park found themselves in the auditorium with a French-speaking crew, a Mao-suited local crew and two French-Chinese interpreters. There was an urgent need to see if Park's structures actually worked. On opening the flight case to start on the assembly, it was discovered that all the two-part nodes connecting the aluminium tubes together had a casting flaw. For the next three hours everybody was busy filing the blip off. By evening, the first 15-metre (50-ft) tower had been pinned together on the floor. It took only two men to lift it upright and set up the outriggers. Park tested it by climbing up the nodes and swinging around on the top.

The Jarre tour in China (*above*) incorporated many of the ingredients of later Fisher Park projects, including lighting specifically designed for television and live recording. Early ideas for the tour included a set of spaceframes, some of which were to hang from the roof and could be moved during the show. Later he and Jarre changed the concept to a set of towers (*opposite left*) which could be used for lighting and sound. Jonathan Park can be seen testing the stability of the structure. Park worked out the detailed design as a Buckminster Fuller-inspired tensegrity system of very lightweight aluminium tubes connected to nodes with quick-release pins. Prototype nodes were cast and tested in the structural laboratories of the Polytechnic of Central London. The system he evolved (*right*) was a modular spaceframe kit of extreme lightness, adequate strength and great engineering elegance.

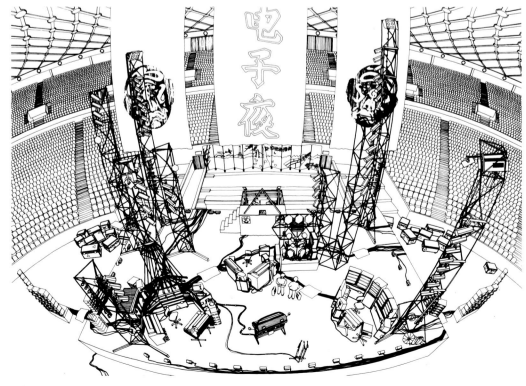

With the exception of the banners at the rear, Jarre's visually extraordinary show was primarily a lighting creation (*left*).

Park's elegant structures were connected together for the first time in Peking after their journey in boxes of amazingly small dimensions, which belied the eventual size of the set (*above*).

Graphic designer Kate Hepburn worked on the show and produced a complete graphic identity, from tickets through the record sleeve to the designs on the scrims hung around the stage and auditorium.

Since *The Concerts in China* tour, Fisher Park have worked on a number of projects with Jean-Michel Jarre. The first was a proposal for a concert outside Buckingham Palace, the centrepiece of which was to have been a big open pyramid made from the geodesic tower structures which Park had designed for China. That project fell through, not surprisingly, given the sensitivity of the site. Earlier Jarre had mounted a show at Place de la Concorde in Paris which involved using giant images projected on to surrounding buildings. In 1986 he asked Fisher Park to devise a show for Houston (*right*) celebrating its 150th anniversary. He played to an audience of around a million with the tall towers of the city as his background, illuminated with giant images and lasers and pyrotechnics. Similar projects designed by Fisher Park for Tokyo (*below*) and New York (1987) failed to come off, but their design for the two 1988 Jarre shows, *Destination Docklands* did. They designed an extensive performance area floating in one of the Royal Docks, with the surrounding industrial wasteland used as screens for giant projections thrown more than 250 metres across the dock.

ULTRAVOX
QUARTET

WORLD TOUR 1982

The next job to come through Britannia Row was the set for Ultravox's indoor 1982 European and American tour. Peter Saville had designed the record sleeve. Ultravox wanted the set to be a three-dimensional version of Saville's design. Fisher and Park's set design used elements from the record sleeve and took the form of a large central structure in false perspective, a series of corrugated screens and a back-projection cyclorama.

Although the set was essentially a collection of theatre-style flats, it had to have its own structural integrity and had to travel. A modular system for the timber and stressed skin panels was devised so that they could be loaded in and out of venues rapidly. By Fisher Park standards, this was a relatively straightforward set, yet marvellously suited to indoor venues. Combined with dramatic and imaginative lighting design, it provided an immediately recognizable and effective link with the overall promotion of the band's latest album – an example of a total media package which includes the set design.

The background tower (*right*) is silhouetted by the deep pink glow of the cyclorama. The drum kit is backlit in cool blue.

The tower is almost lost in a dark blue light at the back of the stage, with the band's backline washed in green. At the front of the stage Midge Ure is highlighted in gold (*below*).

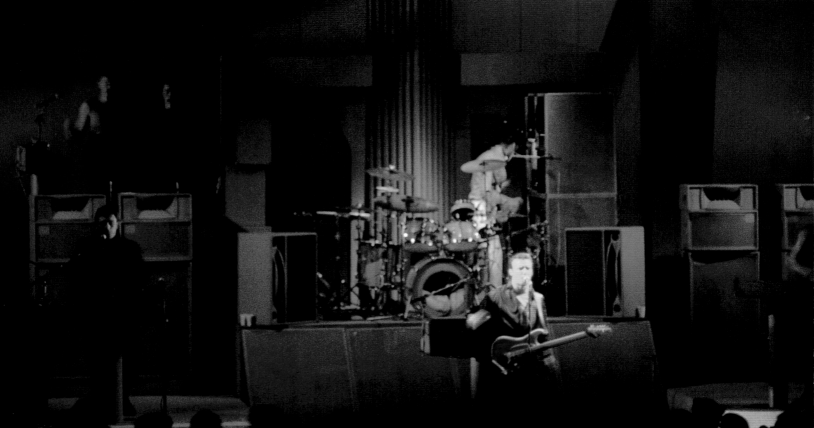

MURRAY HEAD
HEAD SET

TOUR 1983

At the end of 1982 actor-singer Murray Head's manager, Michael Deeny, approached Fisher and Park to design a set for Head's tour in France, where he was a cult chart star. Coming from the theatre, Head felt that it was important to have a set. For this tour he wanted one which had an industrial flavour. He also wanted to be fired out of a cannon during one song. Fisher and Park designed a set faintly reminiscent of the factory set in Fritz Lang's film *Metropolis*.

Park toured this show and manoeuvred the cannon and set in and out of a number of very small halls in France. The cannon itself was built in aluminium, covered with plywood by Fisher, Park and Paul White, a craftsman joiner.

Two years later Murray Head asked them to design and build a set in which he could simulate moonwalking. Made mainly from plywood panels, the set was built as a room inclined at 60 degrees with painted false perspective. Head apeared from the top of the set in a counterweighted flying harness and sang 'walking' around the set.

The centrepiece of the set was a furnace with a fat, vertical chimney (under construction *below right*) which slid forward, rotated and turned into a cannon (*right and below*). At the beginning of one song, clad in an astronaut's suit, Murray Head climbed into the barrel and was apparently fired across the stage to land in a net at the back of the auditorium. Head actually slid down the barrel, out of the back and ran round to the rear of the auditorium to jump into the net as a thunderflash and smoke bomb went off on stage.

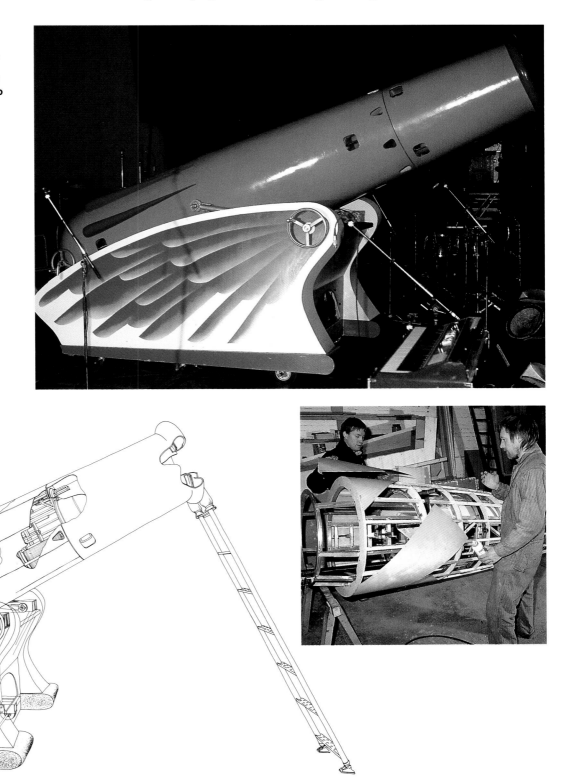

'Winging it' – the Art of the Big Tour

Tours have an organic cycle which flows seamlessly and often sleeplessly from one show to the next. For an indoor show the first trucks, having left the previous location by 2.00 am, arrive at the new venue by 8.00 am. The rigging crew has its first meeting with the venue's management, brief the locally hired additional crew and immediately start establishing the hanging points for lighting, sound and scenery. The chief rigger sets out chalk marks on the floor for the chain hoist positions and the crew up in the roof start anchoring a network of cables and support points directly over them. The chain hoists are modified industrial models: instead of fixing the hoist motor unit in its normal position overhead, the end of the chain is anchored to the roof structure with high-strength nylon slings and the motor unit hangs above the stage floor far below. When the time comes to fly, the motors climb up their own chains, hauling the attached lighting and PA and scenery into position above the stage.

It is much easier and safer for a rigger to take a long coil of rope and haul the chain hook up into the roof structure than to haul up scores of heavy motors and chains – and then let the chains down. This mid-seventies insight was probably Rocky Paulson's – a rigger from San Francisco who had worked with all the major West Coast bands. CM Hoists of California were the first to modify their standard industrial hoist mechanisms for rock shows.

In the early stages of rigging a show, up to 70 chain hoists will be hanging above the stage.

Meanwhile, the electricians will have found the local power supply and wired in enough cables to power the chain hoists. The lighting bars and trusses with their PAR cans attached are wheeled in on trolleys, laid out on the floor in the positions they will occupy overhead, attached to the chain hoists and then hauled up to shoulder height for final adjustment.

At the same time the riggers use the chain hoists in front of the stage to fly the PA units which come in off their trucks at around 10.00 am. If things are going well by then the lighting trusses can be flown into position. By midday the scenery is brought in and similarly flown into position.

By now, the technical crew will have eaten breakfast and started to set up sound and lighting control gear. The band's monitor mixing boards are set up at the side of the stage and any other control gear installed. By 2.00 pm, sound and lighting managers are checking the lighting and equalizing the loudspeakers with white sound to match the

reflection and absorption of the house. By this time the élite band crew, sleeping in buses outside in the loading dock, get out of bed, direct the unloading of the band's instruments and gear and set them up on stage.

By 4.00 pm, everything is in place ready for the sound check which normally starts with the microphones on the drum kit. If there is a warm-up act it is given a few minutes to do its sound check when the headline act has finished its own check. At 6.00 or 7.00 pm the audience comes in while the crew members have dinner.

The show finishes at 11.00 pm or so and in more or less reverse order the crew takes everything out: band instruments, backline and desks, and then enough scenery to allow the lighting and PA to be loaded on the waiting trucks. The scenery and special equipment such as video projectors follow and finally the rigging is taken out of the roof. Because the chain hoists will be needed first thing at the next venue, there is often a second complete set of chain hoists which leapfrogs from venue to venue when a tour has dates a long distance from each other. The practical limit is around 400 miles in the United States; less in Europe with its national border crossings. The crew catches a few hours sleep in a caravan of buses before the 8.00 am start the next day.

Many bands carry out this gruelling programme five times a week with a basic crew of perhaps 40 people. Crew numbers have increased over the years from the time Pink Floyd, with their big shows, had a crew of 25. Today, the average big tour includes the band, their personal and security staff, the production manager, technicians for instruments and the back line and stage sound crew. There will be one lighting technician or more, a front-of-house sound engineer and crew, pyrotechnician and an assistant, generator operators, rigging crews, scaffolders, carpenters, scenic technicians and, when the set is in any way complicated, a series of technical specialists and their assistants for such items as video projectors, cameras and inflatables. Associated with them is the merchandising team, caterers, management and accountants.

Transporting and storing pyrotechnics presents a special set of problems because of strict national safety rules. Normally the stock of pyrotechnics has to be cached in approved stores and only the supply for one show drawn at a time.

In some countries it is necessary to bring in a great deal of additional equipment, simply because it is not available locally: portaloos, fencing, temporary plywood tracks for forklifts. When Pink Floyd played Moscow in 1988 they had to take their own self-contained village: diesel tankers and even refrigerators filled with food. Few of that crew met a Russian.

Outdoor shows follow the same routine, except that the scaffolding on which the scenery, lighting and sound are hung will have been set up by an advance crew ready for the load-in. In a very big show, the band may be on stage in San Francisco, while a second set of scenery is being hung on scaffolding in Los Angeles and a third set of scaffolding is being erected in Phoenix. There may even be a fourth set of scaffolding, en route from Portland to Denver. But because scenery is expensive, most bands try to avoid having a second set.

ROGER WATERS
PROS & CONS OF HITCHHIKING

TOUR 1985–86

Three transparent gauze roller screens were hung in a row in front of a wide projection screen. The effect of depth was achieved by false perspective painting. Images could be back projected on to the screens. The gauzes were rolled up during the show to display the whole width of the rear screen.

The three rollers (*opposite*) showed respectively: the window of a motel room, the rear of the room and an enormous television set. The effectiveness of the show's graphics as a complement to the live performance can be seen *below* and *opposite below*.

Roger Waters toured the multi-media *Pros & Cons of Hitchhiking* around America and Europe in 1985 and 1986. Its theme was broadly to do with middle-class, middle-age sexual angst portrayed as a series of dreams set in a motel bedroom. The show was presented on consecutive nights in cities up to four- or five-hours truck-drive apart.

The set consisted of a 9-metre- (30-ft-) high by 30-metre- (98-ft-) long projection screen tensioned on a lightweight modular box aluminium trussing. It was used as a wide back-projection screen for single or triple images, a mixture of live action filmed by Nicholas Roeg and animation drawn and directed by Gerald Scarfe. In front, hung from overhead rollers, were three 12-metre- (40-ft-) wide transparent scenery gauzes painted in false perspective; from left to right: the motel window, the rear of the motel room and a television set. Film images were seen through the window, the wall and the television. In some sequences the gauzes were flown out, and the picture spread across the 30-metre (98-ft) width of the rear screen. The whole show was controlled by a time code generator which synchronized film, sound replay, quadrophonic effects and cues for the band. The scenery rollers were mounted on wheels so that they could be moved and trucked as single units.

The *Pros & Cons of Hitchhiking* set is perhaps most notable as a demonstration of Fisher Park's ability to come up continually with brilliant multi-medium solutions to the problems of presenting shows on a non-stop basis in different venues.

ROGER WATERS

RADIO K.A.O.S.

WORLD TOUR 1987–88

C ontinuing his development of thematic shows in indoor venues, Roger Waters asked Fisher Park to design the *Radio K.A.O.S.* set for a tour of North America and Europe in 1987 and 1988. The theme on this occasion was of a dialogue between the hero and his imaginary alter ego, a paraplegic boy Billy. A disc jockey introduced the show from a simulated radio studio on a high riser at the rear of the stage and conducted a continuous discussion with Billy's computer-synthesized voice.

Billy's speech and other key words were relayed by a 12-metre- (43-ft-) long running message board across the front of the riser. Film directed by Gerald Scarfe, David Munroe and Jonathan Park was rear-projected on to a 12-metre- (43-ft-) diameter screen, last seen in *The Wall*. The PA was hung above the front of the stage. The whole set permitted the fullest possible integration of visual elements and sound within the confines of indoor venues.

Radio K.A.O.S. in performance (*right*) with the band playing under the message board relaying the words of Billy's voice; the rear projected film can be seen above.

Roger Waters (*below*) in action on the rear riser, shadows combining with ominous film images.

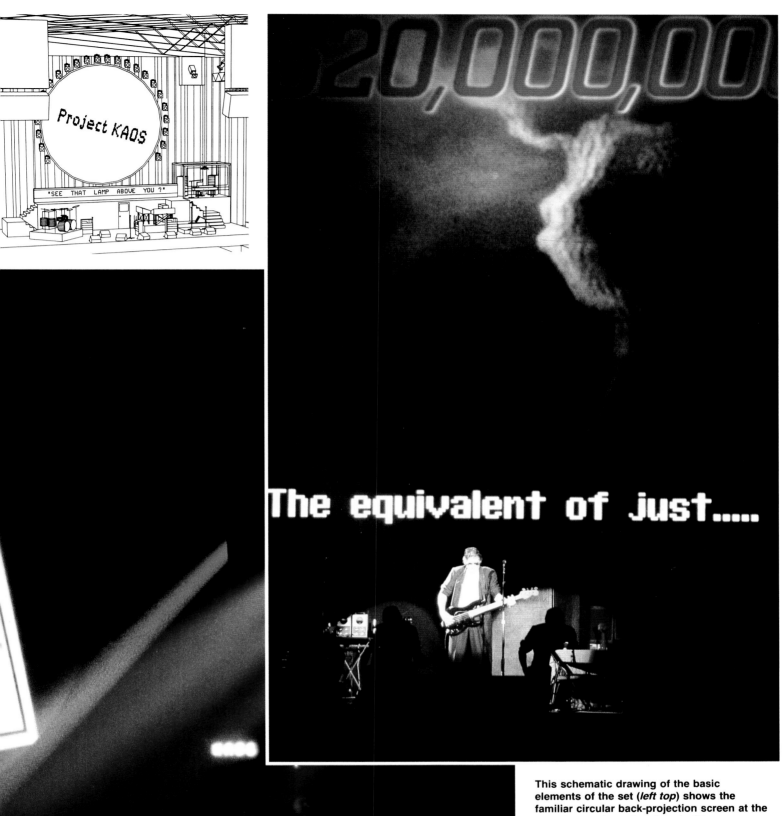

This schematic drawing of the basic elements of the set (*left top*) shows the familiar circular back-projection screen at the rear above a long riser faced with a message board and DJ booth to the right.

Song, message and back-projected images are all integrated on the set (*above*).

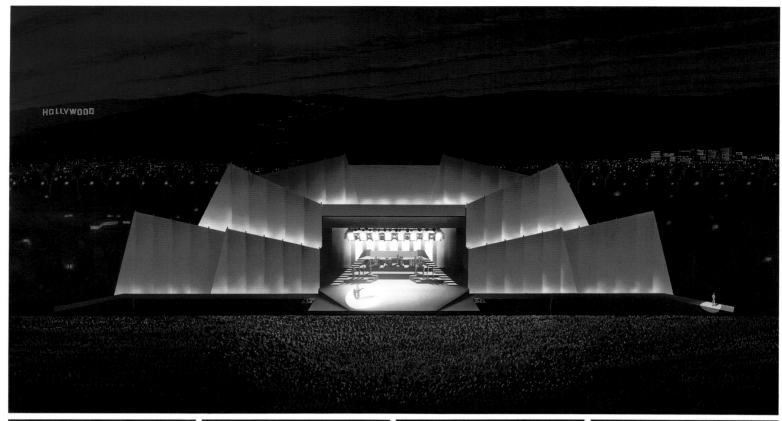

WHAM!

WHAMAMERICA

TOUR 1985

Mark Fisher had worked with Jonathan Smeeton at Britannia Row on projects for Mike Oldfield and Peter Gabriel. Smeeton had then become Wham!'s resident lighting designer; in 1985 he asked Fisher Park to design the set for an eight-city, three-week summer stadium tour around America. Very big distances between dates were involved and it was essential that as much heavy equipment as possible should be hired locally. After intensive discussions, Fisher Park produced a simple and bold design for a set of overlapping sails in a fan-shaped configuration radiating from the stage. They were to be lit by batteries of cyclorama lights in changing colours.

The seven fan sections were erected on a scaffolding framework containing the PA. These acoustically transparent scrims, painted a mid-grey, were each attached at the top to a long pole, hauled up on pulleys attached to the scaffolding and tied down at the base in the fashion of a square-rigged ship's sail.

The mid-grey fans provided a neutral surface for the lighting and colour effects produced by batteries of cyclorama light units (*above and right*); they transform the set from a brightly-lit centre stage to a great, all-embracing structure, as the fans apparently fold out. The square rigging technique was developed by the rock industry to enable scrims in outdoor shows to be quickly pulled down in emergencies rather than, as had been the case on several occasions, cut down when unexpected winds turned into violent gusts.

GEORGE MICHAEL
FAITH

WORLD TOUR 1988

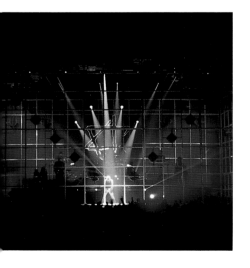

In 1988, when George Michael had gone solo, he asked Fisher Park to design a set for his *Faith* tour of Japan, Australia, North America and Europe. He had the clear idea of singing from inside a cage which gradually opened out during the show – and he wanted a real, rather than a theatrical cage.

Because the cage, its mechanics, curtains and lighting were to be freighted by air, everything had to be as light as possible and capable of being packed in standard 3-metre (118-in.) pallets. The lighting grid and cage walls were fabricated from thin-wall aluminium tubes which were transported in tubular steel carts which then became part of the structure of the stage terracing. The whole set, including lighting, weighed in at 12 tonnes and took a thirty-person crew between six and eight hours to erect, so that the show could be run on consecutive nights at venues up to six hours truck-drive apart.

The mechanisms for lifting the front of the cage were four hydraulic rams pulling ten 8-millimetre (¼-in.) stainless steel aircraft cables. It took a number of shows to get the cage-opening mechanism working smoothly. The side gates were operated by electric linear actuators. Interchangeable stage decking and facing panels were constructed from resin-bonded plywood.

Looking at the contrasting sets for the *Whamamerica* and *Faith* tours, it is impossible to avoid some reflection on the sheer variety of Fisher Park's work. The new generation of rock concert locations has indeed provided unique opportunities for the building of what is, effectively, some of the most impressive architecture of our time.

Fisher Park designed a set which opened with a cage enclosed in curtains bearing the *Faith* logo which was raised to reveal George Michael inside the cage (*left*) with a projection screen across its back. The front section then lifted up to form an open roof over the front of the stage (*above*) and subsequently sections of the side opened out. At the end of the show the cage closed and the curtains were flown in. Jonathan Smeeton designed the lighting so that most of it could be mounted on the cage.

The works of the contributing artists and other key images, which changed during the performance, were enlarged and used to decorate the arena frontage and stage. The main stage, flanked by television screens relaying performances and specially commissioned films, was 18 metres (59 ft) wide and connected by a 50-metre (164-ft) walkway to a second stage used for performances during changeovers. These were effected rapidly by using four rolling platforms for the equipment of succeeding bands.

The concert provided Fisher Park with the opportunity of using potent and already public graphic imagery to reinforce the polemical message underlying the performances.

Annie Lennox and the Eurythmics open the concert (*above*).

George Michael performs against the background of the image of Mandela dominating the centre stage (*above right*).

The 100-metre (328-ft) stage frontage (*right*) was built as a gigantic hoarding which displayed scaled-up polemic artworks and stage graphics commissioned to celebrate Mandela's 25 years of imprisonment. Jenny Holzer's video image shows on the flanking screens and Malangatana's 'Eyes of the World' looks down on the second stage.

Bob Geldof's 1985 *Live Aid* was responsible for something like a revival of the enormous rock festivals of the sixties and early seventies – here with live audiences limited by the 70,000 or so capacity of stadiums, but with extended audiences via television of perhaps half a billion. The formula, however, remained the same: a miscellany of star and up-and-coming groups playing a song or a short set for some worthy cause.

Fisher and Park were very much committed to the cause represented by the first and second Nelson Mandela tributes at Wembley in 1988 and 1990. But what was technically important for them was being confronted with the special needs of television. Rock is not a subtle medium and television has its own challenges: the tyranny of the quick cut between three standard shots, the need for continuous action and, in many countries, the extent to which the political point of view can be expressed. For the *Mandela* concerts, the set designers and the television director had to enable the polemic to read clearly, but not so strongly that it would be cut or bowdlerized by television censors in countries receiving the transmission.

Fisher Park's approach was to use political statement for the inevitable long shots and polemic art in the backgrounds to close-ups of the performers. Producer Tony Hollingsworth suggested that they invite political artists to contribute work for the stage surroundings. This was a new departure for Fisher Park but, in the end, they commissioned a number of international artists opposed to apartheid, including Sue Coe, Keith Haring, Ralph Steadman, John Muafangejo and Malangatana Ngwenya.

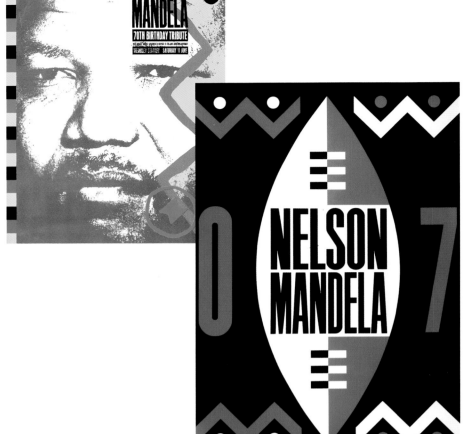

NELSON MANDELA 70TH BIRTHDAY TRIBUTE

WEMBLEY 1988

The programme cover by graphic designers 4i incorporated the most famous icon of Mandela (*above left*).

Kate Hepburn's logo (*left*) was used by 4i for a pair of large self-adhesive posters which formed the running borders for the stage.

The main stage graphics were based on a set of super-scale images from John Muafangejo and Mary O'Shaughnessy paintings; here they form the background to the group Farafina (*below*).

NELSON MANDELA INTERNATIONAL TRIBUTE
FOR A FREE SOUTH AFRICA

WEMBLEY 1990

For the second Mandela concert, celebrating his release from prison, the graphics were developed by 4i using images drawn for the 1988 concert, including the black-and-white handshake by John Muafangejo and emblems by Cheryll Park, which were also used on programmes and posters (*right*). The stage banners (*below*), mounted on three-sided rotating frames, 10 metres (30 ft) high, were turned for each group's performance, reinforcing the political message to the worldwide television audience.

NELSON MANDELA • AN INTERNATIONAL TRIBUTE FOR A
FREE SOUTH AFRICA
SPECIAL WEMBLEY STADIUM COMMEMORATIVE EDITION
APRIL 16 1990 • £6.00

CONTAINS COMMEMORATIVE POSTER
ONLY AVAILABLE AT WEMBLEY
BUY ONE NOW!

LIBERTAD PARA SUDAFRICA

南アフリカ を 解放する

LIBEREZ L'AFRIQUE DU SUD

FREE SOUTH AFRICA NOW

ROLLING STONES

STEEL WHEELS

WORLD TOUR 1989–90

When the Rolling Stones agreed with Canadian promoter Michael Cohl to stage a tour of the United States in 1989, they had not played together in public since 1982. They then had toured with a set which was notable mainly for its use of huge painted scrims designed by Kazuhikde Yamazaki. The edges of the scrims were shaped to the profile of a guitar, a car and the American flag. Patrick Woodroffe had worked on the show as lighting director. The band asked him to advise them about the new set for the proposed tour.

Early discussions centred on making some kind of reference to the environment and the need for a tough, memorable and visually exciting set. Woodroffe wanted to see if it was possible to do away with the traditional roof and the lighting trusses over the stage. It was a sketchy brief, not a vision of what the set might *look* like. Jagger shopped around exhaustively for designers. He finally shortlisted Mark Fisher and Paul Staples, designer of the 1988 Pink Floyd tour set.

The *Steel Wheels* set in the Los Angeles Coliseum makes a dramatic sight against the background of the 'permanent' architecture of the city.

Keith Richards, Mick Jagger and Bill Wyman (*opposite*) on stage during the *Steel Wheels* tour.

These two early Fisher Park concept designs for the *Steel Wheels* set (*above and right*) were eventually developed to become the complex set (*below and far right*).

Mark Fisher produced a series of sketches which illustrated a future in which twentieth-century high technology had become redundant. As part of his presentation he used a big colour picture of a NASA shuttle-launch platform: his point was that it was already obsolete, despite the fact that NASA was still using it. Yet it was possible to feel nostalgic about it and enjoy its evocation of the rawness of an industrial city. Fisher's presentation had an immediate impact on the band. They had a clear idea of what they would look like in performance. The design team started work immediately. The next three weeks saw intense creative design discussions between production co-ordinator Michael Ahern in New York, Fisher Park and Woodroffe in London and the Rolling Stones in Monserrat.

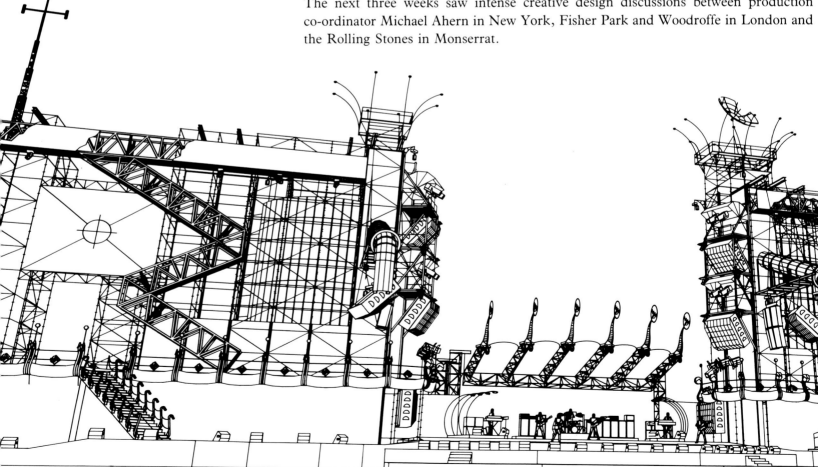

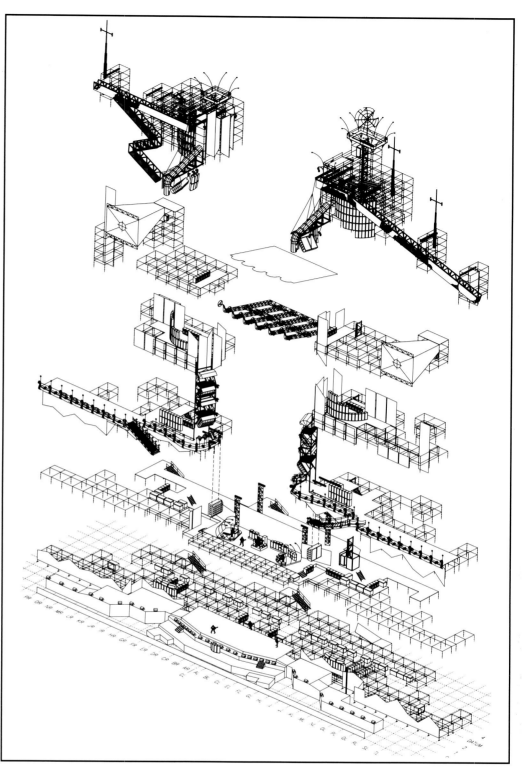

Fisher Park organized the set as two big scaffolding towers on either side of the stage, with the 20-metre (66-ft) PA columns and the 6-metre-by-8-metre (20-ft-by-26-ft) back- projected video screens built into them asymmetrically and higher than usual. The band was placed under a low, cantilevered roof. The towers carried Patrick Woodroffe's custom-built lighting system: banks of lamps with scrolling coloured gels in what looked like giant egg crates aimed down on the stage. Beside these, facing out towards the audience, were two grain-elevator snoots which carried followspots and their operators.

The set was designed to stretch across the end of any stadium in the United States and ended up 93 metres (305 ft) wide, 20 metres (66 ft) deep with an average height of 21 metres (69 ft), some of the set reaching heights of more than 35 metres (115 ft).

They argued their corners, exchanged ideas and established the broad architectural, lighting and construction concept. Ahern was going to direct the tour, so he had to be convinced that the design was practical. Woodroffe had worked with Fisher Park on Roger Waters' *Pros & Cons of Hitchhiking*. They spoke the same design language and both had long experience on the road with touring shows. Woodroffe's approach to lighting design is bold and emotional but it is also sensitive to the need to integrate with the scenic design.

The *Steel Wheels* design was a collaborative undertaking, because Jagger was closely involved in the detailed conceptual discussions as a team member, rather than as a distant client. Within a few weeks other people had joined the team, notably sound director Benji LeFevre. He had worked for a number of big groups and with Fisher Park on George Michael's *Faith* tour. The gradual assembly of the team and its plans demonstrates what a co-operative effort a tour has to be.

LeFevre proposed to use the revolutionary Showco 'Prism' system of interlocking PA cabinets which he had used on the *Faith* tour. He also proposed other practical ideas, such as establishing a floor level below the stage for the rows of amplifiers, to make building, running and striking the show more efficient. He was also very concerned that there should be no obstructions to the even spread of sound to the audience.

Fisher and Park made several models; the third one was approved and work started on construction of the set. The final design was based on a number of sources, including visually memorable industrial structures such as steelworks and refineries – and the ideas of architects like the American Bruce Goff, who used *found* materials for many of his buildings. There was also a literary source in the writings of novelist William Gibson, whose work Fisher introduced to Jagger. The cities of his stories are collages of obsolete layers of technology added to old buildings.

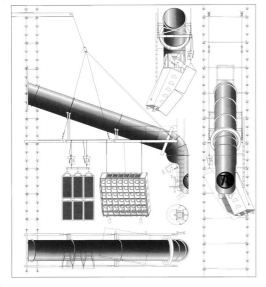

The snoots (*top and above*) were a major feature of the set. Based on grain-elevator chutes, they actually carried followspots and their operators for the duration of the performance. Sound director Benji LeFevre had been told that the snoots were acoustically transparent and rapidly had to devise a 'snoot-defeat' sound system.

A section through the stage (*right*) shows Patrick Woodroffe's custom-built egg-crate lighting system which eliminated the need for the traditional lighting bar across the stage.

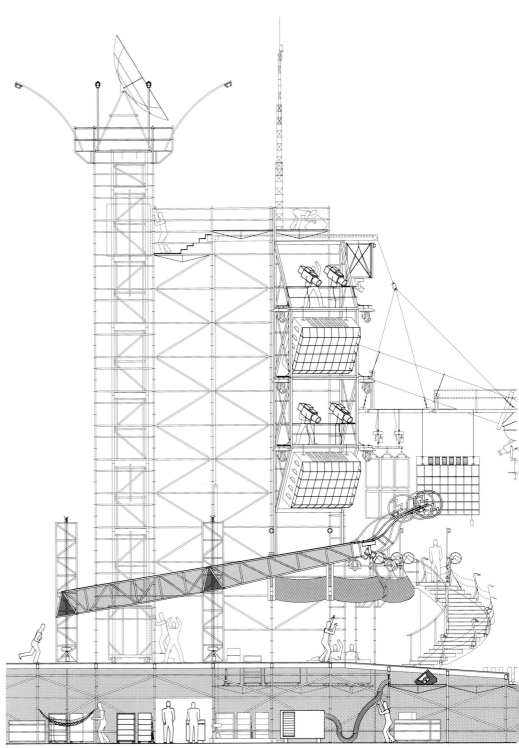

Mick Jagger runs a sound check (*right*).

Computer drawings of the fractured compact disc motifs for the leading edge of the stage roof (*below*).

A detail of the balcony (*bottom*) shows the swagged netting.

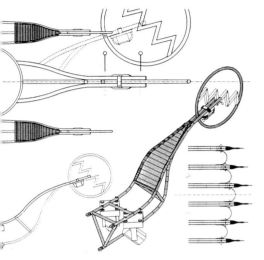

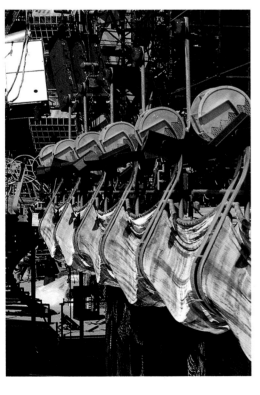

Gibson's work has its visual parallel in David Snyder's sets for the cult Ridley Scott film *Blade Runner*, with its imagery of malevolent skies, crumbling ziggurats and occasional flares from distant industrial complexes.

In the early sixties the visionary Archigram group had celebrated the promise of technology. Fisher Park's set was an ironic comment on that promise. It looked back from the future at the visual consequences of Archigram's thinking and discovered a romantic, ruined technoscape of decayed industrial bridges, gantries, girders and stairways, interwoven with *fin-de-siècle* architectural detailing. The stage set was conceived as a multi-level structure on which the band could perform. In 'Sympathy for the Devil', Jagger appeared on a tower 23 metres (75 ft) above the set, then disappeared in an explosion of flames to reappear mysteriously on stage for the next number. During the song 'Honky Tonk Woman', Angie and Ruby, two inflatable women almost as tall as the set, were blown up from the balconies, where they rocked gently to the music.

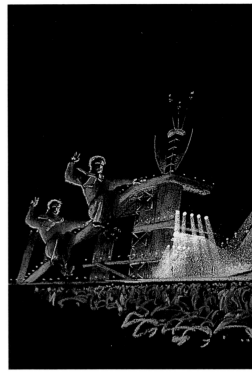

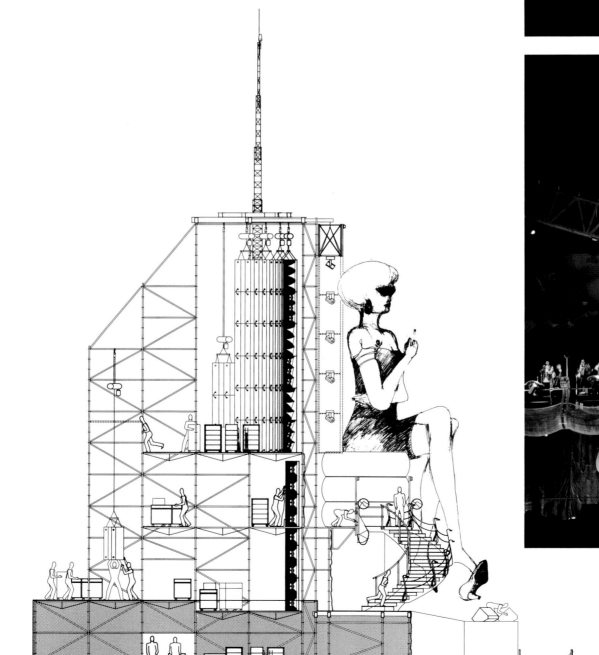

A computer section through the set with Angie inflated; the PA stack is behind her (*opposite below left*).

Angie appears for her three-minute spot (*opposite below right*).

An early concept sketch (*far left*) shows the original proposals for the use of the inflatables.

Ruby inflated for a rehearsal (*below left*); both inflatables had to be designed with great care to avoid charges of sexism.

Mick Jagger on the balcony (*left*) during 'Honky Tonk Woman'; Ruby's right leg is visible in the background.

Keith Richards and Ron Wood on stage (*below*) with menacing, enigmatic sections of the set visible behind.

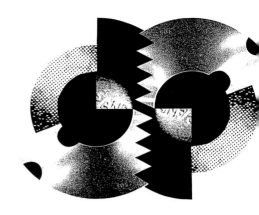

The PA and much of the scaffolding was faced in scrim painted with the circular images developed with Mark Norton of 4i (*above and above right*). These were derived from the shapes of smashed compact discs, circular-saw blades and perforated metal. Additional graphics were also projected on to the stage set from the sound mixing tower in the middle of the audience.

Like much of the work of graphic designers 4i, these images were generated, distorted, merged and coloured on computer. They were also used in some of the promotional and merchandising material for the American and Japanese legs of the tour.

Pyrotechnics were an integral part of the *Steel Wheels* spectacle (*opposite above and right*). At the end of the show the whole frontage of the set structure appeared to catch fire in a mass of flames and explosions. Such a display seemed to set the appropriate final seal to a concert held in a specially created environment of movement and dissolution.

During the show, Woodroffe's lighting changed mood from malevolence to romance, from evil to good, and the set was illuminated with explosions and cascades of flame. This set and all its associated lighting, sound and generating equipment had to be loaded in and out of thirty-three cities over a fifteen-week period. The set had to be constructed to take a lot of punishment. *Steel Wheels* went out with a travelling crew of two hundred people and close to eighty trucks. Temporary crews of up to one-hundred-and-fifty were hired for each performance. The shows started in September 1989 in Philadelphia and toured the north-east of America, then across the Midwest to the West Coast and across the South to Florida and finally, during December, in covered stadiums in the northern states and Canada. It was necessary to have two sets, each run by seventy-person crews with twelve 14.6-metre (48-ft) trucks leapfrogging venues. A universal production team with three semi-trailers worked on each of the shows. In addition, four duplicate scaffolding teams, each with ten trucks, set up the basic structure for the shows in advance. Two 12-metre (40-ft) trucks carried pyrotechnics.

Patrick Woodroffe's lighting underlined and reinforced the look of each song (*following pages*). From number to number it completely changed the character of the set, from fundamental, raw, gutsy industrial dereliction, through looming malevolence to serene romance.

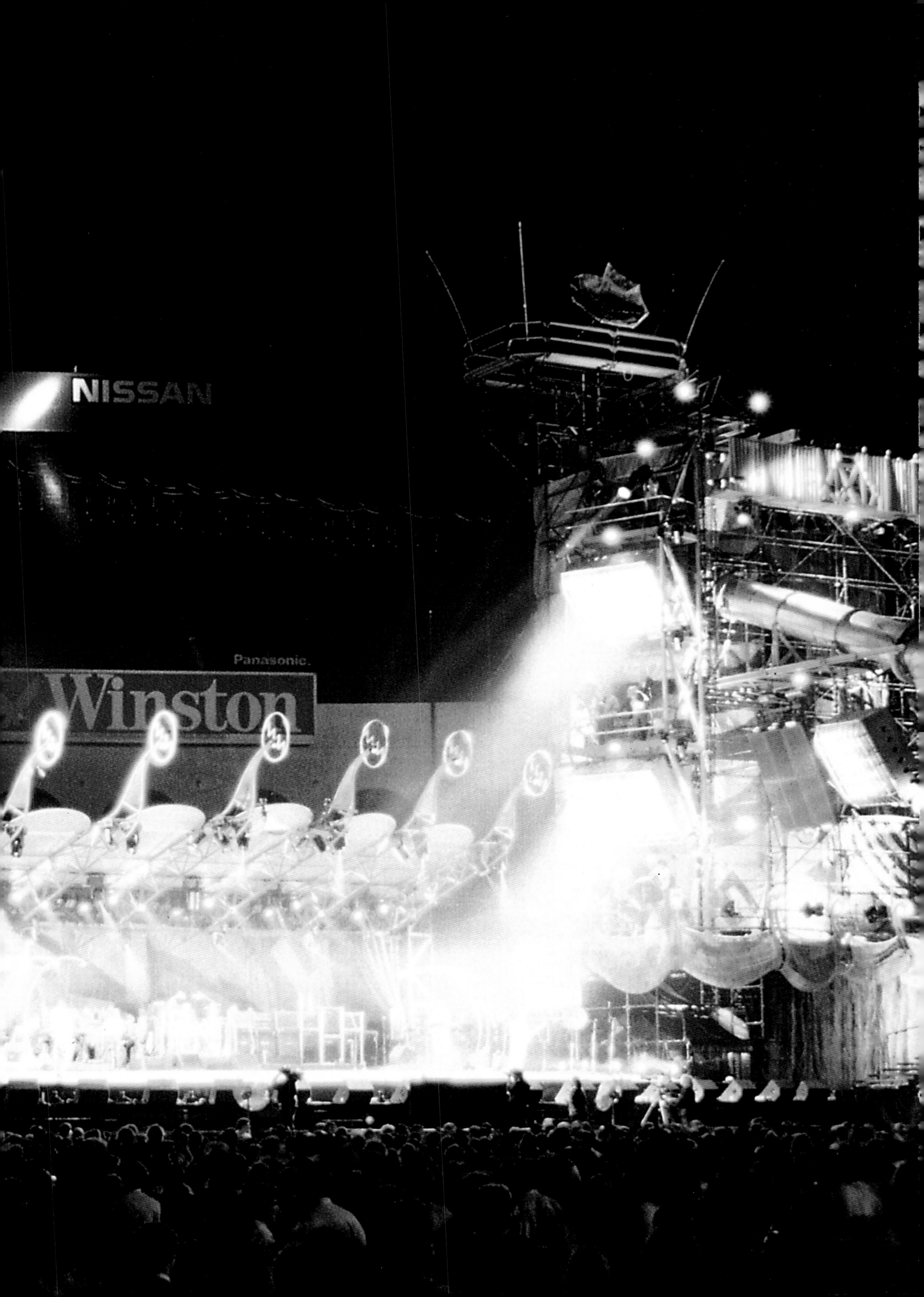
NISSAN
Panasonic.
Winston

ROLLING STONES
URBAN JUNGLE

EUROPEAN TOUR 1990

Fisher developed a less complicated set and faxed some preliminary drawings to Jagger with the suggestion that *Urban Jungle* might be a good title. His early designs (*below*) included huge inflatable jungle animals. When Mark Norton of 4i became involved, he conceived an idea of urban decay in terms of vicious dogs instead of a zoo of beasts and drew a crazed creature which became the graphic motif for the show (*right*). In a series of planning sessions, many of them conducted in drawn form via fax, the design team came to the idea of a corroding industrial technology overgrown by a fluorescent jungle, from which wild dogs emerged to savage the performers. Three of the four inflatable dogs (*left*) were sculpted by Paul Wright. All were made by Rob Harries' Air Artists. The new configuration had the players on stage with a 10-metre- (33-ft-) high header above, two scrim-covered towers on either side, one encasing the lift and an open framework of scaffolding either side of the curving stack of the red and white striped PA above scrim wings. The video screens were freestanding at either end in an orthodox configuration.

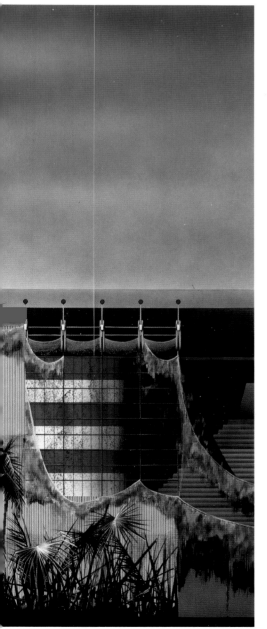

The European version of the *Steel Wheels* set had to be designed for smaller stadiums, many of them a long distance from each other. In some northern summer venues the show would be performed entirely in daylight. This presented particular problems for lighting designer Patrick Woodroffe. His broad strategy was to use essentially white light and pyrotechnics for the beginning of the show and to bring in a startling colour introduction when it was sufficiently dark for the full effect of coloured lighting to register with the audience.

The band approved the design for *Urban Jungle* and Fisher watched it go up for technical rehearsals in Edwin Shirley Trucking's yard near London's City Airport where it remained erected for two weeks. The band saw it for the first time in Rotterdam and rapidly came to the conclusion they didn't like it. 'Too theatrical', said Jagger. Production director Michael Ahern immediately hired the Ahoy exhibition hall and over the next two days the scrims were repainted as rusty yellow corrugated iron. The show started touring with this revised temporary set and Fisher immediately started designing a new set combining the show's rabid dog motif with images inspired by American Indian symbols used in a video sequence for the song 'Terrifying'. He had the design approved in Hanover and the new scrims were ready for the Lisbon show two and a half weeks later.

JANET JACKSON
RHYTHM NATION 1814

WORLD TOUR 1990

With its array of aluminium towers, platforms, staircases, ladders and ramps, the set had a distinctly industrial appearance, reminiscent of the power station in which part of the *Rhythm Nation* video was filmed (*opposite above and below*). The 12-metre (39-ft) towers supported industrial cranes festooned with lights, beneath which were platforms carrying followspots. The towers themselves were decorated with fluorescent lights set behind metal grilles, and contained other lights which rose and fell on tracks. The stage set include an 9-metre- (30-ft-) long telecaster board set beneath a dance platform (*left*).

The Fisher Park computer schematic for the set (*below*).

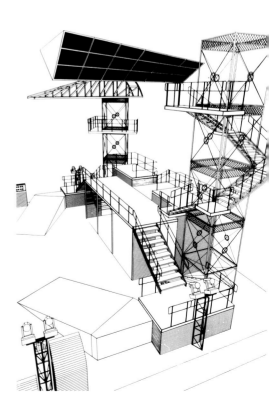

Janet Jackson wanted a stage show which picked up the themes of her *Rhythm Nation* video drama. The video was a tightly choreographed musical set in a monochromatic world of decaying cities, rooftops and factories. Fisher and Park watched it, made some sketches and started discussions over a preliminary model. They worked on the design with lighting director Roy Bennett.

The songs on the album explored Jackson's attitudes to social problems like poverty, drugs, illiteracy and racial prejudice. She believed that music and dance could unite people and give them the power they need to overcome the social problems which prevent them achieving their potential.

The second half of the show featured songs from the *Rhythm Nation* album. The lighting which had concentrated on the performers was turned on to the aluminium structures which became menacing cityscapes, factory interiors and discothèques. Jackson and her dancers moved through this moody landscape, lit from unexpected directions by lights concealed behind grilles, and buried in ventilator shafts and revolving cowlings. A telecaster board was used to present abrupt slogans from the *Rhythm Nation* lyrics.

The stage was always located at one end of the arena, but it was designed to be seen in the round. The band played partly hidden under the dance platform. Jackson and her six dancers moved above, behind and in front of them, using the open towers and staircases alternately as backgrounds and foregrounds.

TINA TURNER
FOREIGN AFFAIR

EUROPEAN TOUR 1990

At the opening of the show the stage went black and a 9-metre- (30-ft-) long staircase descended from the roof. Turner entered at the top of the stair 6 metres (20 ft) above the stage and descended during the first number. The staircase then flew out to reveal the band behind (*see plan opposite*).

The climax of the show was Turner's ride out over the audience on her 'claw' (*left*). Its passenger platform was disguised as a small thrust stage built on to the front of the main stage (*below*). At the end of her last song the 'claw' retracted and the staircase flew in again for Turner to make her exit.

Tina Turner's *foreign affair* tour was designed to play in both indoor and outdoor venues. The stage set was designed so that the playing areas could be used on their own in indoor arenas without the PA wings and roof used in outdoor stadiums. Turner wanted the stage to reflect the key qualities of her music: a tough yet glamorous design which could handle both over-the-top moments of raw rock and moody intimate ballads.

The main features of the design were strong, curving, raw-aluminium forms. The hard, polished surface of the metal was broken up by rivets and grilles which added sparkle and texture to Patrick Woodroffe's lighting. The fascia of the roof floated above the stage, with nacelles on its leading edge concealing six followspots.

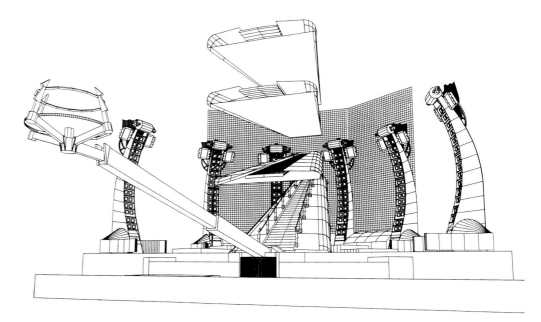

WHITNEY HOUSTON
I'M YOUR BABY TONIGHT

WORLD TOUR 1991

The production design for her 1991 world tour was conceived around Whitney Houston and her six-piece band, accompanied by four backing vocalists and four male dancers. The final design came out of a series of discussions between Fisher Park and the lighting designer Marc Brickman.

Brickman brought two strong ideas to the project. The first, a development of his work with tracking Vari-Lites on Pink Floyd and Paul McCartney shows, was to rig pairs of Vari-Lites mounted back-to-back on inclined spars. The second was to use a full-width back-projection screen to display powerful graphic and video images.

The main performance area was downstage in front of the band, where it extended on to a plexiglass-covered thrust stage with Vari-Lites underneath. A 6-metre- (20-ft-) wide balcony 3 metres (10 ft) above the stage, spanned the drummer and the percussionist to provide a second performance area. The two areas were linked by curving staircases on either side decorated, like the balcony, with aluminium and copper balustrading. When Houston was on the balcony it tracked forward to within 2.4 metres (8 ft) of the front of the stage to prevent her being upstaged by the dancers below.

A range of graphic projection images were prepared for the show by the designers 4i in London. The subjects ranged from stills of Houston and her family singing in gospel choirs, to cartoon illustrations and graffiti graphics. In a typical sequence, a song opened with full-screen graphics which cross-faded through several images during the instrumental introduction.

A rear-projection screen 6 metres (20 ft) high by 18 metres (60 ft) wide was rigged upstage of the band above the rear of the balcony (*below left*). A combination of slide projectors and video projectors delivered a seamless image of uniform brightness across the full width of the screen.

When the vocal started, live video projection was mixed from a four-camera system. When Houston was on the balcony her own dramatically enlarged live image appeared behind her (*left*).

Six Vari-Lite spars stood on the stage floor. Two tracking units, each containing two Vari-Lites were mounted on each spar. The units tracked up and down the full length of the spars, lighting the performers from a number of angles (*below*). The tracking system, developed by John McGraw at Planview in Los Angeles, was fully programmable for acceleration and tracking speed. Many motion effects were possible, including starting the lights at different times, yet having them reach their stop positions on the same cue.

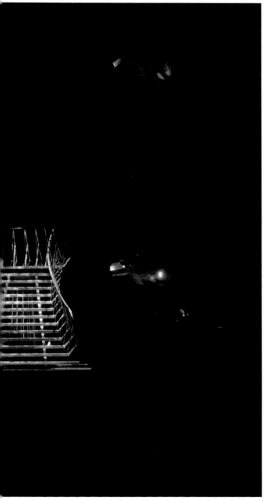

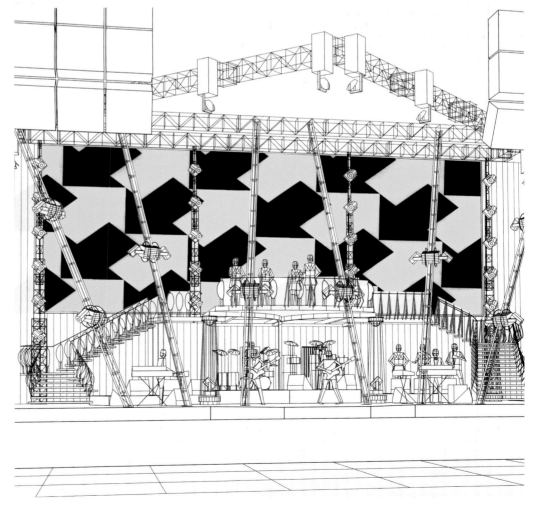

U2
ZOO TV
OUTSIDE BROADCAST

WORLD TOUR 1992–93

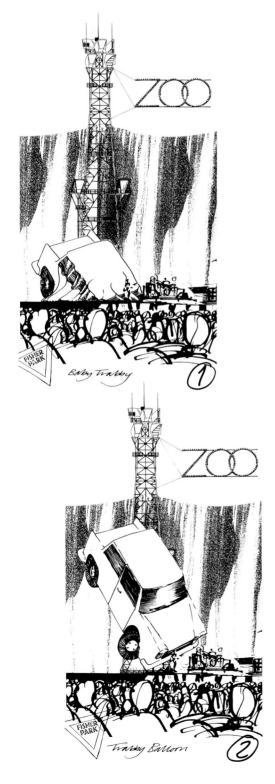

Many of the design proposals for the *ZOO TV Outside Broadcast* tour were discussed with the band via fax. Fisher developed his drawing technique from the beautiful but obsessively detailed drawings of his earlier years, through coloured and black-and-white impressions of a show in performance, to a kind of drawing specifically executed to maximize the current limits of fax transmission, making it possible to conduct detailed design discussions directly from the studio. There comes a time, however, when it is necessary to discuss the three-dimensional model, so Fisher and Park travelled very extensively with the nearly 3-metre- (10-ft-) wide model from London to wherever the band was playing.

One of the later developments of the set design was an ingenious scheme retaining the projection curtains stretching across the end of a stadium with a big tower to one side festooned, like the area surrounding the stage, with Trabant cars concealing lights and a secondary performing area extending far into the audience.

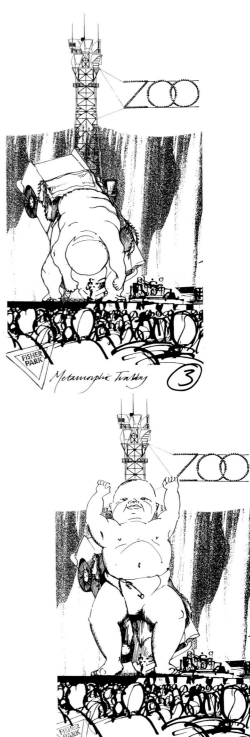

Among U2's original ideas for the set for their 1992–93 stadium tour of the United States, Japan and Europe was a plan to work with the alternative circus company Archaos. Fisher Park developed a design in which the anarchic acrobats and clowns would perform in the afternoon on, around and above the stage and also from girders over the audience (*above*).

Later proposals included a series of 18-metre- (59-ft-) long curtains suspended on 25-metre- (82-ft-) high masts right across the end of the stadium to serve as projection screens. Another sketch adopted the idea of U2's lighting director, Peter Williams, using key words from songs to reinforce the music (*left*). Fisher Park also sketched an inflatable Trabant rising out of the stage floor (*opposite left*), metamorphosing into a baby (*above*).

ROGER WATERS
THE WALL

BERLIN 1990

In late 1989, rock show merchandiser Mick Worwood asked Roger Waters to stage *The Wall* for Leonard Cheshire's Memorial Fund for Disaster Relief. The war hero's aim was to raise five pounds for each of the dead of the Second World War – about £500 million. Waters and Fisher Park had been talking around the idea of a revival of the 1980 show. Two months later, when the Berlin Wall was demolished, they decided to stage the revival in Berlin in early June 1990.

Negotiations started with the mayors of East Berlin and West Berlin for a one-night performance on the Potzdamer Platz, the no-man's land on the East Berlin side of the wall. East Berlin was in political and bureaucratic turmoil and nobody in government had any experience of staging rock shows. For five months there was great uncertainty about who should or even *could* give permission.

Finding sponsors for the show was difficult, even though Roger Waters had committed the royalties from the album of the show to the Memorial Fund in perpetuity.

The Teacher puppet makes its first appearance (*above*).

The preparation of the site (*right*).

A wall-building rehearsal (*inset right*); the two rectangular openings are for video screens and one of the scrim coverings for the PA is visible on the right.

The layout of the Potzdamer Platz for the Berlin *Wall* (*below*); the wall stretched across the neck of the site, leaving a quarter of the 10-hectare (25-acre) site behind it for stars, crew, catering, wardrobe, props, parking and

television transmission. The towers in the foreground are for lighting and sound.

The 25-metre- (82-ft-) high wall stretched 80 metres (591ft) across the site, each end stepping irregularly down to the ground. In front ran a long forestage, wide and strong enough to take limousines, motorbikes, military trucks and the Marching Band of the Combined Soviet Forces. Two truck-mounted cherry pickers with spotlight gun turrets were located in front of the forestage and two were located behind the wall, forming part of the mechanical choreography.

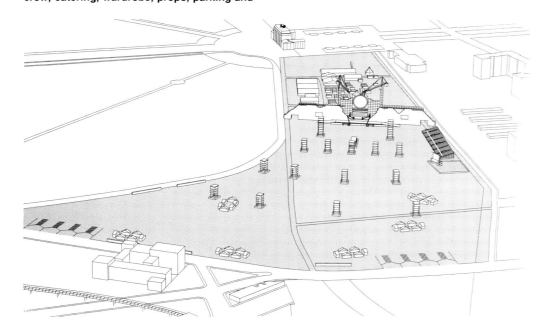

The cardboard bricks used in the original production of *The Wall* were not strong enough to support the increased loadings of a wall almost twice the height. Polystyrene bricks had been discounted on cost and ecological grounds. But one of the German production assistants, Werner Graf, discovered that they could be made from fire-retardant polystyrene foam by the German firm Welkisch Papiergrosshandlung. They manufactured 2500 tongued-and-grooved bricks (each measuring 75.5cm × 60cm × 150cm (29¾ in. × 23⅝ in. × 59 in.) and afterwards recycled them as construction insulation. A wall of polystyrene bricks 18 metres (59 ft) high would have blown over unless tied back to some kind of structure. Local regulations insisted that the wall should be able to resist a 40 mph wind – and wind speeds were almost that high during rehearsals. Park had decided to use vertical masts as the supports, after discussing a variety of other solutions with engineers Whitby and Bird. Californian construction manager, Chris Teuber, proposed using East Berlin builders' hoists with slim triangular lattice truss towers. The wind masts were fixed at 6-metre (20-ft) intervals across the centre opening in the wall and painted black to blend with the rest of the set.

The bricks had to be tied back at regular intervals to the wind masts and scaffolding to stabilize them. A fundamental question was how to fix the bricks securely and yet allow a fast progressive collapse. Teuber came up with the simple solution of tying a piece of cord around a 30-centimetre- (12-in.-) long wooden dowel, and laying the dowel in the top groove of a brick before the next course was placed on top. The cord was then tied back to the nearest wind mast or scaffolding upright. The 600 bricks of the middle section had to be laid in 47 minutes. The tightly scripted show was controlled by time code. This ensured perfect synchronization of the music, sound effects, live action and television transmission.

The first four courses, up to above head height, were laid by German extras from the stage. Then a 12-metre- (39-ft-) long lintel truss faced with simulated bricks was swung into place, creating an opening. Performers moved through it until it was sealed up at the end of the first half. The upper part of the wall was laid by stage hands working from a bridge rising behind the wall.

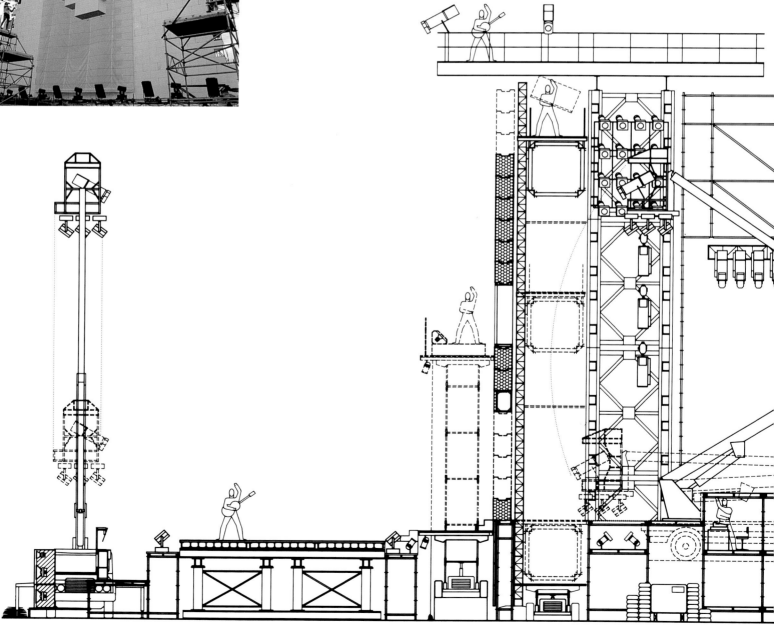

Fisher and Park had planned to use scissor lifts for the wall-layers' rising platforms. It turned out that none of sufficient height were available for hire. So a 40-metre- (131-ft-) long bridge was built across the stage behind the central opening. The bridge and lifting towers were constructed from readily hired components. The 20-tonne bridge was lifted by hydraulic motors to provide fine control and reduce noise.

Two 12-metre- (39-ft-) high PA towers were located behind the wall on either side of the stage, disguised by acoustically transparent 70 per cent gauze panels painted to simulate brick courses. Two big video screens were positioned either side of them.

Behind the PA were four levels of scaffolding platforms for brick storage. The two inflatables were stored on platforms behind the top of the wall on each side.

The band played on a stage behind the wall. Behind them, under a roof, was tiered staging for the 80-piece East Berlin Rundfunk Symphony Orchestra and the 150-person East Berlin Radio Choir. The bottom of the 15.2-metre (50-ft) diameter circular back projection screen aligned with the front edge of this roof. Behind the choir was the tower for the 70-millimetre (2¾-in.) cine projector focused on the back of the circular screen.

On either side of the stage, built into the scaffolding supporting the brick storage, were two 50-metre- (164-ft-) high tower cranes with 30-metre (98-ft) jibs. A mobile telescopic crane was parked behind on stage left. The cranes were used to fly in sections of the wall, support the Teacher puppet and, in the second half, to raise a 40-metre- (131-ft-) long lighting truss above the front of the wall.

Instead of the puppet of the first *Wall*, the Mother was now a Scarfe cartoon painted on the translucent covering of a light box (*opposite left above and below*).

This computer section through the stage (*below left*) shows from left: followspots on cherry picker, forestage with lift, the wall, wind mast, rising wall-builders' bridge, with its towers, performing area, orchestra and choir terracing with roof and circular back-projection screen above.

The circular projection screen frame was supported by elaborate scaffolding on either side (*below*); only two partial rehearsals of building and demolition were allowed to conserve bricks (*bottom*).

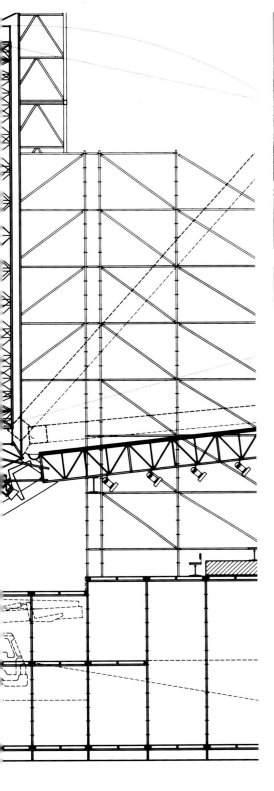

Bryan Adams in rehearsal for 'Young Lust' (*right*).

The crowd begins to assemble for the show (*below*). Two hundred thousand tickets were printed, but it is estimated that 250,000 people were actually present.

In January, when planning for the event started, all the large companies had committed their sponsorship budgets for the next year. Eventually the show cost around 10 million to stage.

Through January and February, Fisher Park worked on the visual and mechanical design, producing computer renderings and drawings. Park, with television producer Tony Hollingsworth and local production manager Sigi Paul, effectively took charge of operations until the East Berlin permit arrived on 20 April and a full production team could be assembled. At first there was no proper budget and many of the people with whom Fisher Park usually worked were engaged by the other big touring shows running at that time.

By April the project had passed the latest practical start date for a June performance and the show date was moved to 25 July. The team had now been joined by production co-ordinator Keith Bradley and technical manager Chris Teuber. Fisher Park had worked with Hollingsworth on the two *Mandela* concerts and with Teuber on the original *Wall*. Sigi Paul, a Berlin architect and theatre producer, managed the labyrinthine process of getting the permit. Bradley, who had previously worked with Elton John and INXS, began to put the production team together.

In mid April the permit to stage the show finally arrived. This left two and a half months to get it built and rehearsed, a ridiculously short time for such a massive undertaking – one of the greatest concerts ever.

'Another Brick in the Wall, Part 2' (*below*); Gerald Scarfe's Teacher cartoon is displayed on the big circular projection screen behind.

'Another Brick in the Wall, Part 2'; the Teacher puppet looks menacingly over the top of the wall (*following page*).

Cyndi Lauper (*inset following page*).

The Mother image appeared for the song
'Mother' on the light box (*below*) and on the
circular screen (*above*). The song was
performed by Sinead O'Connor.

'Good-bye Blue Skies', an appropriate song
for one of the most dramatic lightings of the
set (*right*).

Joni Mitchell, James Galway and the Band
(*inset right*).

This drawing of the middle section of the wall (*below*) shows the Teacher puppet (*preceding page*) inflated and dangling over the wall. In the actual performance the puppet's torso was supported by a mobile crane from behind. The Teacher's long cane by the right-hand tower crane was also used to fly the Mother brick.

This projection of graphics by Scarfe (*bottom*) accompanied the song 'Empty Spaces'.

Graphic images by 4i design group for the hotel scene, in which Roger Waters sings from a three-dimensional hotel room. The room, built into the wall, was visible through sugar-glass windows. It remained hidden by a flap painted as if part of the wall, until the time for the song. 4i's images for this part of the show were deliberately based on contemporary cartoon drawing techniques, self-consciously coarse, ugly and crude.

The graphic images were projected from five 19-metre- (62-ft-) high towers sited 100 metres (330 ft) out in the audience, using Pani projectors. The three inner towers also carried 7-kilowatt Xenon cine projectors which projected sequences of synchronized film on to the middle section of the wall.

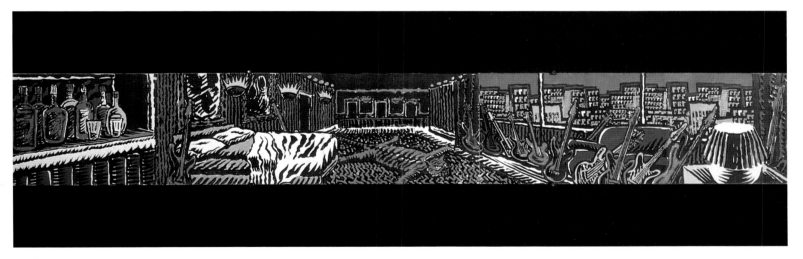

The graphics of a ravaged city, designed by 4i, were projected across the full width of the wall (*above*). The hotel room can be seen to the left.

Jerry Hall sings 'Wanna Take a Bath?' (*inset above left*). She did, in fact, deliver this number from the lower part of the set.

Waters had made some minor changes for the new performance: adding or dropping a song, extending some instrumental sections and having arrangements written for the new live backing orchestra and choir. The original running order and concept remained essentially the same. In 1979–80, *The Wall* had been a milestone in the staging of live rock shows. But with an undemonstrative band, long, idiosyncratic guitar improvisations and projected animation in place of strutting performers, it was not good television. The Berlin version was to be watched by a live audience of more than 250,000 people and broadcast live to thirty-five countries to an estimated half billion people. The cameras needed continuous live action. In addition, the Potzdamer Platz site called for a set twice the size of the original. This all meant that, to keep the continued attention of both television and live audiences, there would have to be a shift in scale both physically and in terms of action: the storyline had to be strengthened into a clear narrative with an unambiguous message.

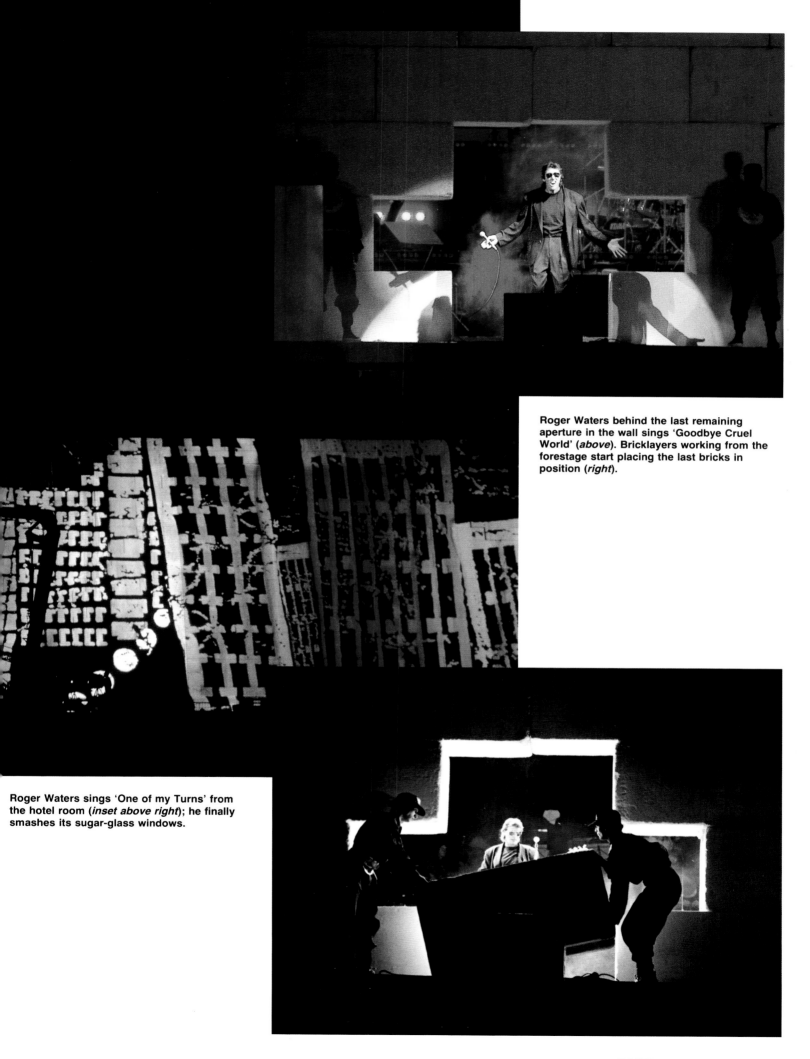

Roger Waters behind the last remaining aperture in the wall sings 'Goodbye Cruel World' (*above*). Bricklayers working from the forestage start placing the last bricks in position (*right*).

Roger Waters sings 'One of my Turns' from the hotel room (*inset above right*); he finally smashes its sugar-glass windows.

Projection of real Berlin Wall graffiti (*opposite left*); these were selected from photographs and montaged together to create this image.

At the beginning of the second section Waters sings 'Nobody Home' from a chair on the forestage – in front of the completed wall (*opposite right*).

Images were montaged from press cuttings of a variety of twentieth-century conflicts across the wall for the 'Vera' number, sung by Roger Waters (*below*).

Fisher and Park had already roughed out several ideas for changes to the set, notably the hotel room scene. This was now located in a three-dimensional hotel room set high in the wall, hidden until the beginning of the scene by a brick-painted lift-up flap. The original Mother inflatable was replaced by a Mother brick, a large light box concealing a Scarfe cartoon which fitted into a triangular notch in the top of the wall.

Scarfe's images had been designed to suit the scale of the original arena performances. Fisher and Park wanted to strengthen the narrative to make the show read as a more contemporary event – and to give it more of their own style. They wanted a new strength and toughness and worked with the design group 4i to produce the new graphic images.

The feeling of the 4i designs was in strong contrast to Scarfe's quirkily scratchy line work and sharp violence: the scale of Potzdamer Platz called for less subtlety. The new graphics were mostly symbolic rather than literal – thick, heavy, simple, relentless and frequently distressed with cracked and broken edges. They worked well with the Scarfe imagery and were immensely strong when they were used in their own right: an abstract, nightmarish, ravaged cityscape projected across the wall during the hotel room scene, the sombre list of names of the dead which spread across the wall and turned into a field of crosses and the 13-metre- (43-ft-) high by 150-metre- (492-ft-) wide phrase 'BRING THE BOYS BACK HOME', which came across with uncompromising force both live and on television.

The Helvetica Bold Condensed type of 'BRING THE BOYS BACK HOME' (*top and left above*) had never before been used on this scale; it was computer generated, printed out, distorted and copied many times before being hand-painted and turned into projection transparencies.

The sombre list of names of the dead from the World Wars (*above*).

The consequences of conflict (*left*).

Images of fascist architecture were distressed and montaged for these projections of the rally scene (*opposite above*).

To save costs and cope with the doubled scale, the Pig was redesigned as a monster head to break through the top of the wall (*opposite centre and below*), its spotlight eyes glowering over the audience. Gerald Scarfe drew a new cartoon and sculptor Paul Wright created the 1:12 scale model for fabrication as an inflatable by Rob Harries' Air Artists. The size of a five-storey house, the Pig was painted by Keith Payne in one of the pre-war airship hangars at Cardington.

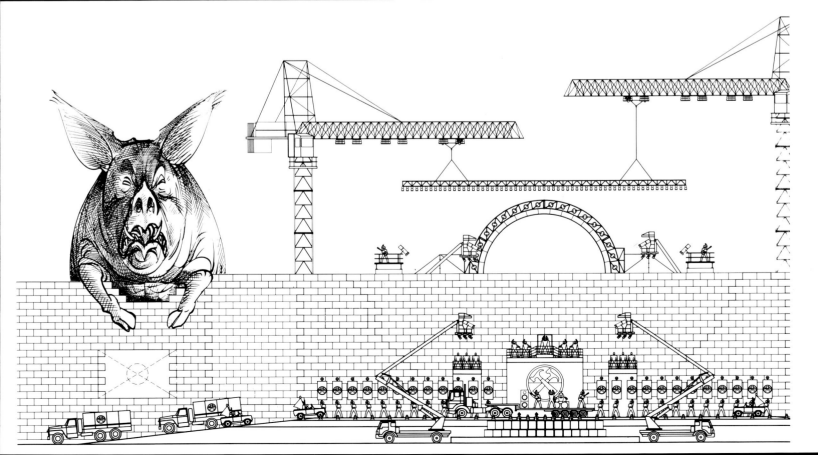

The fascist rally graphics projected on to the wall, with The Scorpions performing from a flat-bed truck (*opposite and above*).

Roger Waters sings 'Waiting for the Worms' (*above right*).

Thomas Dolby, in flying harness and oversize Teacher costume, is suspended above the forestage (*below left*).

Albert Finney underneath the heavily padded judge's costume for the trial scene (*below right*).

The rally and trial had originally been illustrated by large-scale projected movie animations by Gerald Scarfe. Like the rest of the Scarfe graphic imprint, they would remain a fundamental element in the performance, augmented by additional footage, some of it from the film of *The Wall*. But with an under-occupied Soviet army still resident in the city, Waters was enthusiastic about turning the rally into a live choreography of Russian tanks and soldiers. The local Soviet army command balked at tanks, but hiring troop carriers, Generals' jeeps and military marching bands turned out to be a matter of amicable negotiation with them. Anxious to foster artistic collaboration between the newly united countries, the radio orchestra and choir and many extras and crew were hired from East Berlin.

The trial sequence was reworked as a long vignette played by a group of star actors in fantastic Scarfian costumes: musician Thomas Dolby was dangled down the wall in flying harness wearing a twice life-size costume modelled on that of the Teacher.

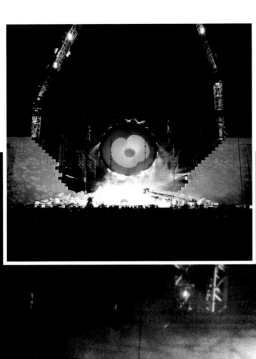

The extras were ranged along platforms on the scaffolding wings and the 15 brick-layers positioned on the long bridge. At the cue the bridge began to descend and the bricklayers progressively pushed off each succeeding course in a great cascade. Because of the need to conserve the relatively fragile bricks there had been only two partial demolitions before the show – although there had been many wall-building rehearsals.

With 'Tear Down the Wall', the vast edifice which had served as symbol, set and vast projection screen began its progressive collapse.

The demolition spectacle begins (*inset above*).

The cast assembles on the bridge for the final bow (*inset left*).

The end of alienation (*inset right*).

The final demolition of the wall (*below right*).

The Wall had been created in only two-and-a-half months – with access to the Potzdamer Platz site for only the last four weeks. By normal rock show standards that was an impossibly tight schedule: ideas, mechanisms, choreography, lighting, pyrotechnics, sound and logistics had all to be tested out and co-ordinated.

Although Fisher Park were closer to the reins of control than is normally the case, the experience of *The Wall* reinforced their belief that rock'n'roll design is a team business, an integration of creative activity from many different sources. However seductive the theoretical positions of the post-war avant-garde may be, the creation of rock architecture is dependent on imagination, appropriate technology and, above all, on teamwork. Perhaps, when a final assessment is made of the work of Fisher Park, they will be seen as the creative unit which made one of the most practical contributions to fugitive and mobile architecture. Everything they have designed has had to prove its worth in one of the most demanding of contemporary environments – the rock concert.

ILLUSTRATION CREDITS

Unless indicated otherwise below, all photographs are by Mark Fisher, courtesy Fisher Park Limited, and all illustrations are by Mark Fisher, with some technical drawings by Francis Chee. Appreciation and thanks are due to the following owners and photographers for the use of illustrations:

4i Limited 38 *above*, 38 *centre*, 43 *above*, 43 *centre*, 52 *above left* (*Steel Wheels* logo development), 52 *centre left* (*Steel Wheels* logo), 61, 85; AP/Wide World Photos 15 *above* (Woodstock Festival, 16 August 1969); Glenn Brown 22 *above left*; Adrian Boot/Retna Pictures Ltd. 39 *above* (Annie Lennox and Tracy Chapman), 39–40 *above* (George Michael); Simon Conolly 10–11 *above* (Mark Fisher, Simon Conolly and Piers Gough, 'Inflatable Submarine', 1971), 11 *above right* (Piers Gough *et al.*, 'Mother of the Arts', 1967), 11 *upper centre left* (Simon Conolly and Mark Fisher, 'Dynamat', 1971); Peter Cook 12 *above* ('Instant City Airships', 1971); Peter Davies 11 *below* (Chrysalis, 'Desert Fun Environment', 1971); Marc Garanger/Jean-Michel Jarre and Francis Dreyfus Music 26–27, 28 *above left*; Gaylord Gilbertson 18 *below left*; Graceland, a division of Elvis Presley Enterprises, Inc. 13 *above* (Elvis Presley in concert *ca.* 1956); Kate Hepburn 28 *below right*; Hipgnosis 17 *below left*; Laister Dickson 72; Deborah Loth 43 *below*; Dominic Michaelis 9 *below* (Dominic Michaelis and Jonathan Park, 'Solar Balloon', 1972); Millar & Harris/Powell Moya Partnership and *The Architects' Journal* 12 *below left* (Sir Phillip Powell and Hidalgo Moya, 'Skylon', 1951); Tony Mottram 78 *inset*, 88 *above right*, 93 *below right*, 94 *below left*; Jose Nava 9 *above* (Graham Stevens with Jonathan Park, 'Transmobile', 1971); Ortner & Ortner 12 *below right* (Haus-Rucker-Co, 'Oasis No. 7', Documenta 5, Kassel, 1972); Jonathan Park 16, 18 *centre left*, 18–19; Michael Putland/Retna Pictures Ltd. 38 *below* (Farafina), 93 *below left*; Ron Reid 15 *below left* (Knebworth Festival, 1978); Ringling Bros. and Barnum & Bailey Combined Shows, Inc./C.P. Fox Collection 13 *below*; Chris Rodley/ICA 39–42; Paul Slattery/Retna Pictures Ltd. 6 *above*, 77, 79–82, 90 *above*, 91 *above*, 95 *below right*; Peter Smith 24 *left* (Mark Fisher *behind* and Jonathan Park *in front*), 72–73, 72–73 *inset*, 76 *above*, 76 *below*, 78, 79 *above*, 79 *below*, 82 *inset*, 83, 84, 86 *above left*, 86 *above right*, 86–87, 87 *above*, 87 *below*, 88 *above left*, 88–89, 90 *below*, 91 *centre left*, 92, 93 *above left*, 93 *above right*, 94 *above left*, 94–95, 95 *above right*; Mick Treadwell 21 *above*; UPI/The Bettmann Archive 14 *above* and *below left* (Beatles, concert in Shea Stadium, 15 August 1965), 15 *upper centre* (Isle of Wight Festival, 28 August 1970); Manfred Walther 90 *centre left*, 90 *centre right*; Steve Weinberg 91 *centre right*.

AUTHOR ACKNOWLEDGMENTS

This book is dedicated to all people who have been involved in making these projects happen. Rock'n'roll shows are ephemeral events and the record of the huge amount of effort that goes into creating them is fragmentary. This book is an attempt to collect together some of the fragments, and I would like to thank everyone who made the shows possible.

I have particularly to thank Mark Fisher, Jonathan Park, Deborah Loth, Mark Norton, Patrick Woodroffe, Brian Croft, Wilf Scott, Benji LeFevre and others who have spoken frankly about their years in a hard business.

FISHER PARK ACKNOWLEDGMENTS

The execution of rock'n'roll shows is a collaborative undertaking. During the fifteen years that we have been in the business, we have had the pleasure of working with many gifted people, from artists and truck drivers to production managers and road crew. We are well aware that without their vision and support the projects which have been illustrated in this book would never have been realized.

The artists with whom we have worked have sometimes risked their wealth on these crazy projects. Foremost amongst these is Roger Waters, who, with Pink Floyd, gave us the opportunity to build *The Wall* in 1979. Among the many production staff and technicians who made that show possible, the project relied heavily on the tenacity of Graeme Fleming, a man who taught us a great deal about the practical side of rock'n'roll touring. Ten years later, Michael Ahern brought together a production team for the Rolling Stones' *Steel Wheels* tour. It contained some very experienced people, and we had the opportunity of working with them on the most ambitious touring show of the decade. Our thanks are due both to the artists, who paid for everything, and to the crews, who reassembled our designs show after show during the tours.

In the end the success of our work depends to a large extent on the lighting designers with whom we work. We have been fortunate in working closely with some of the best in the business, and the photographs reproduced here would be nothing without their skills.

BIBLIOGRAPHY

Ant Farm, *Inflatocookbook*, 1970.
Arcidi, Philip, 'Lights, Steel and Stones', *Progressive Architecture*, p. 21, Connecticut, December 1989.
Banham, Reyner, 'A Home is not a House', *Art in America*, April 1965.
Brown, Mick and Loder, Kurt, 'Behind Pink Floyd's Wall', *Rolling Stone*, pp. 14–16, 16 September 1982.
Brown, Patricia Leigh, 'Guerilla Architecture: The Stones Set' *International Herald Tribune*, 7–8 October 1989.
Bullock, Chip, 'The Wall Comes Tumbling Down', *Show Technology*, pp. 24–27, Texas, July/August 1990.
Coleman, Ray, *The Legend of John Lennon*, show catalogue, 1990.
Cook, Peter (guest editor), 'Unbuilt England', *Architecture and Urbanism*, No. 83, October 1977.
Conolly, Simon, Davis, Mike, Devas, Johnny, Harrison, David and Martin, Dave, 'Pneuword', *Architectural Design*, pp. 257–278, June 1968.
Conolly, Simon, and Fisher, Mark, 'Stretch-it-yourself', *Architectural Design*, pp. 452–453, July 1972.
Egashura, Shin, 'Fisher and Park', *The Japan Architect*, Vol. 64, No. 4, p. 169, 1990.
Fisher, Mark, 'Design for Entertainment', *British Architecture*, pp. 94–107, Academy Editions, London, 1982.
Fisher, Mark, 'It's Only Rock'n'Roll, the Steel Wheels North American Tour', *Architectural Design*, March/April, 1990.
Fisher, Mark, 'Nice Ideas For Structures . . . and Fun', *Architectural Design*, pp. 457, London, July 1974.
Fisher, Mark, 'Play Net', *Architectural Design*, pp. 792–793, London, December 1974.

Fisher, Mark, 'Responsive Dwelling Project', *Architecture and Urbanism*, p. 60, Tokyo, October 1977.
Fisher, Mark, 'Rock Concerts in Stadia: The Rolling Stones in Concert 1989–90', *Steel Construction Today*, pp. 182–185, London, 4 July 1991.
Forcer, Catriona, 'Rolling Stones: Steel Wheels Across the States', *Lighting and Sound International*, pp. 28–32, Sussex, November 1989.
Free South Africa, show catalogue, 16 April 1990.
Gannon, Louise, 'Pop Goes the Wall . . . Again!', *The Daily Mirror*, p. 3, London, 23 July 1990.
Gelly, Dave, 'Up the Wall', *The Observer*, 10 August, 1980.
Grossweiner, Bob, 'Sold Out', *Performance*, pp. 4–6, 8–10, USA, 22 June 1990.
Herzog, Thomas, *Pneumatic Structures: A Handbook for the Architect and Engineer*, pp. 56, 134, 186, Crosby Lockwood Staples, London, 1977.
Hopkins, John, 'The Pink Floyd versus Psychedelphia', *International Times*, January 1967.
Ibelings, Hans, 'Rock and Roll op een Veredelde Schroothoop', *Archis*, p. 5, Belgium, March 1990.
Leasing, James, 'Making The Steel Wheels Roll', *Performance*, pp. 58–62, USA, 22 June 1990.
Lethby, Mike, 'Rock'n'Roll Theatre on the Grand Scale', *Lighting and Sound International*, pp. 15–20, August 1990.
Lyall, Sutherland, 'The Fun Side of Inflation', *Design Week*, p. 9, London, 6 March 1992.
McElvoy, Anne, 'Borderline Success', *The Times*, p. 21, London, 23 July 1990.
Moen, Debi, 'Whitney Houston's World Tour', *Performance*, p. 10, Texas, 8 November 1991.
Mitchell, Tony, 'Five Young Architects', *Building Design*, pp. 14–15, London, 27 September 1974.
Neale, David, 'Le Maitre On Tour', *Lighting and Sound International*, pp. 39–42, Eastbourne, September 1990.
Niesewand, Nonie, 'Fisher and Park', *Vogue*, pp. 188–193, London, December 1990.
Park, Jonathan, 'The Prismatic Staging Gantry', *Tubular Structures*, pp. 4–5, London, June 1979.
Rockwell, John, 'Floyd's Great "Wall"', *New York Times*, 2 March 1980.
Sandall, Robert, 'Wall-to-Wall Entertainment', *The Sunday Times*, London, 15 July 1990.
Shane, Grahame, 'Architectural Drawings', *Bennington Review*, p. 43, Vermont, September 1979.
Smith, Giles, 'A Set Way of Doing Things', *The Independent*, p. 15, London, 15 June 1990.
Stevens, Graham, 'Pneumatics and Atmospheres', *Architectural Design*, pp. 165–174, London, March 1972.
Sudjic, Deyan, 'Instant City', *Blueprint*, pp. 30–33, September 1989.
Sutcliffe, Phil, '. . . And Pigs Will Fly!', *Q*, No. 48, pp. 72–76, September 1990.
Sweet, Fay, 'Fantasia builds on Rock', *The Independent*, p. 15, 2 January 1991.
Thom, Cleland, 'Kids . . . it's time to learn those ropes', *Islington Gazette*, 26 July 1974.
Wall Berlin 90, The, Show catalogue, July 1990.
White, Jim, 'Saturday Light Fever', *The Independent*, p. 23, London, 4 July 1991.
Williams, Mike, 'Patrick Woodroffe', *Lighting Dimensions*, p. 42, New York, November 1991.